THE
POWER
OF
POSITIVE
STUDENTS

THE
POWER
OF
POSITIVE
STUDENTS

Dr. William Mitchell
with Dr. Charles Paul Conn

William Morrow and Company, Inc.
New York

To my wife Carolyn, who has given me thirty-two years of unconditional love; and to my sons, Billy and Michael, from whom I learned the importance of giving unconditional love.

Copyright © 1985 by H. William Mitchell

Library of Congress Cataloging in Publication Data

Mitchell, William, 1932–
    The power of positive students.

    1. Education, Rural—South Carolina—Sumter County.
2. Socially handicapped children—Education—South
Carolina—Sumter County.   3. Achievement motivation in
children.   4. Mitchell, William, 1932–   5. School
superintendents and principals—South Carolina—Sumter
County—Biography.   I. Conn, Charles Paul.   II. Title.
LC5147.S6M57   1985   371.96′7′09   84-27233
ISBN 0-688-04492-1

Printed in the United States of America

First Edition

1 2 3 4 5 6 7 8 9 10

Book Design by Richard Oriolo

INTRODUCTION

I became acquainted with Dr. William Mitchell, then a superintendent of schools in South Carolina, when he invited me to speak at a "Positive Thinking Rally" involving his entire school system.

Intrigued by the novelty of a school superintendent in a large district having such a meeting, I accepted his invitation. The meeting, held in a huge amphitheater, attracted thousands. Classes had been dismissed for the afternoon and practically every student and many parents packed the large hall.

Enthusiasm ran high as awards were given for high scores in scholarship, leadership, personal involvement, and attendance. Even though I have spoken at many achievement gatherings of highly motivated persons, I was astounded by the upbeat spirit I sensed in this great crowd of students and parents. These people, young and old alike, were actually excited about education.

I had been reading criticisms of our educational system. Everyone, it seemed, was convinced of a lower level of academic achievement and attendance, and a higher level of drop-outs, hostility toward teachers, vandalism, and absenteeism. This gathering gave a totally different impression, however, and statistics confirmed that integrating the concepts of positive thinking into the curriculum had significantly increased academic achievement, reduced absenteeism, and heightened the desire to become good students. From everything I observed that afternoon and subsequently, I concluded that the teaching of positive thinking had succeeded in turning around many students who had been desultory or even hostile toward their education in the past.

Dr. Mitchell's search for solutions to the widespread underachievement that plagued him and his fellow educators ended when he realized that all of the problems confronting the educational system stemmed from one cause—low self-esteem.

Aware that among the chief causes of low self-esteem are negative thinking, lack of self-confidence, and not believing in one's self, Dr. Mitchell conceived and developed a comprehensive, systematic program to help *all* students and employees learn to believe in themselves, to be self-confident, and to learn to like themselves. This program became known as the "Power of Positive Students."

Scarcely ever have I encountered a positive-thinking program as well thought out, as scientifically executed, or as carefully implemented as this one. I am deeply impressed by it. As one afflicted with feelings of inferiority and poor self-esteem as a youth, I am particularly sensitive to the importance of caring, love, encouragement, and praise from those whose lives touch mine. Encouragement and praise growing out of love and caring have the power to change a life, and that life may in turn change others.

The Power of Positive Students program is an important development in American education. It has the potential to influence the lives of millions—the lives of the youths in our schools and of the adults in the communities they serve. It could, I believe, improve the state of education in the entire country. Indeed, a change has already begun in many schools. The degree of success the program achieves will depend upon the support it receives within each school from students, parent-teacher groups, civic and professional organizations, and local businesses.

As a parent and a positive thinker, I recommend this interesting, informative book to every family and educator. This program has the power to restore to American education the emphasis on self-respect and self-esteem that characterized our schools in the past.

—NORMAN VINCENT PEALE

1

In 1978, I was superintendent of a school system that seemed to be going nowhere. Conditions were bad, morale was worse, student performance was below the expectations of all of us who cared. In Sumter, South Carolina, virtually everyone was unhappy with the public schools, and that included me.

I had come to Sumter County four years earlier, excited by the challenge of a new job as school superintendent. I had arrived with some emphatic ideas about education, and with great confidence that every problem could be solved if one simply worked hard enough. I have been accused of having hyperactive adrenal glands—maybe it's true. Certainly I believe hard work, by itself, will whip most any problem.

After four years on the job, that premise was being sorely tested. We had made many improvements in the Sumter County schools, to be sure, but beyond a certain point additional gains I so badly wanted had eluded us. Some of the goals I had set for my administration were as distant as when I arrived, and no amount of hard work and long hours had made much difference. I was totally frustrated, stuck in a giant-sized professional rut, and I couldn't find a way out.

Understanding the situation requires knowing something about Sumter County, South Carolina, and something about me as well. We were, in a way, well matched: nothing particularly glamorous or sophisticated about either of us. Sumter was a hardscrabble sort of place, and I was a hardscrabble sort of person.

Sumter County is in central South Carolina, far removed culturally from the Deep South aristocratic tradition of coastal Charleston or from the newly affluent resort areas of Hilton Head and Myrtle Beach. The Sumter psyche and life-style reflect both the mountainous Piedmont region and the coastal area. It is a place where people work hard for a living, always have, always will.

In Sumter County, I served School District Two, a district covering 676 square miles with very sparse population. The students, roughly ten thousand of them, were 60 percent black and 40 percent white. About one-fourth of the kids were affiliated with Shaw Air Force Base, the area's largest single employer. It was a county whose per capita income was well below the national average and whose native population was mostly rural.

Although it had its share of dedicated teachers, District Two traditionally had not been regarded as a good school system when I went there in 1974. None of its fifteen schools was accredited by the Southern Association of Colleges and Schools, the regional accrediting agency. Student misbehavior had been such a problem that because of the high number of suspensions the district had been cited as an example of discipline problems in a national publication. The military families assigned to Shaw Air Force Base had been highly vocal in their criticism of the school system, justifiably concerned about inadequate facilities, poor student performance on national tests, improperly certified teachers, high levels of absenteeism by both teachers and students, continuous vandalism, and a lack of elective courses in the curriculum.

None of these deficiencies discouraged me when I arrived in Sumter to take the position as superintendent. To the contrary, I rather relished the challenge of it, rolled up my sleeves, and went to work. There were plenty of concerned parents and teachers in Sumter, and the most obvious and urgent problems were solved. The physical plants were improved, teacher certification procedures were upgraded, and all of the schools were accredited by the Southern Association of Colleges and Schools.

So things got better—up to a certain point. But I soon learned that only the most glaring deficiencies were easy to correct. Problems such as inadequate buildings and manpower shortages could be solved with infusions of money. New courses could be developed, hiring practices could be revised to guarantee a better-trained faculty—all those solutions were obvious, and the people in District Two worked hard to get those jobs done. But the root problems didn't go away. No matter how hard we worked, we still had a school system that was not teaching its kids how to be successful men and women. We still had too many students who left school without ever discovering the joy of learning, too many youngsters who slipped through our classrooms without even scratching the surface of their inherent capacities for growth and development.

And it seemed to me that it was getting worse. No matter how many shiny new buildings we built, the basic failure of District Two—the failure to energize and challenge students, the failure to teach them how positive and exciting life can be—haunted and frustrated me. It was a rut from which we couldn't seem to escape.

Like thousands of public school educators before—and since—I was stalemated. My idealism, along with my smile, was beginning to wear thin. For a person who had always taken great pride in his ability to meet any challenge, my professional impotence was especially galling. I had pushed all the buttons and pulled all the levers at my disposal, I had done it by the book, I had put to work all the administrative strategies I knew, and none of it had made much difference. The sad fact was still this: I was presiding over ten thousand students who were for the most part turned off by the educational process and whose performance showed it.

That spring of 1978, as I wrote my annual report to the South Carolina Department of Education, my disillusionment came into focus. It was not just District Two in which the condition of education was so bleak, but in most communities and most public school systems throughout the country. No wonder the burn-out rate—and the drop-out rate—is so high among public school teachers and administrators! Every time school officials get together, our conversations revolve around the dismal state of our schools: declining achievement test scores and college board exam scores, high rates of failure and dropouts, increasing absenteeism, loss of many of our most capable teachers to other professions, the high cost of maintenance due to vandalism, reports of increased discipline problems and violent crime.

All these problems have produced a massive loss of confidence in the traditional concept of public schools as a great opportunity to prepare children for fulfilling and useful adult lives.

But what to do about it? I was tired of the constant

sense of failure, but none of my strategies was working. As I looked for help from other sources, I realized that around the country, dozens of programs have been developed to reverse the erosion of public confidence in the schools. Most of them have been expensive, and most of them have not worked. John Goodlad, dean of the College of Education at UCLA, recently admitted, "We are forced to conclude that much of the so-called educational reform has been blunted on the classroom door."

Still, I discovered there was a way out of the rut in which we found ourselves in Sumter District Two, and it came not from an educator's administrative handbook nor from a book on educational theory. It came from a single concept that effective teachers and parents have understood for years. When we rediscovered that simple concept and integrated it into our educational programs, things began to change in Sumter County.

2

Too many of the students in Sumter County considered themselves unable to compete with kids from more impressive backgrounds—so they didn't try. They feared they would fail at tasks that were intellectually ambitious—sure enough, they usually failed.

To kids with that conviction, school is never much fun. The classroom is a place to be endured or avoided whenever possible. A class is an instrument of boredom; a book is a symbol of a kid's own ineptitude; a simple conversation with a teacher is a minefield of potential embarrassment. The tragedy is that most school-age kids in America today have a similar mindset! It is the exception rather than the rule, not just in rural, lower-income counties in South Carolina but in the middle-class suburbs, in the homes of well-heeled and well-educated parents, as well as in inner-city and rural areas.

Few things are more crippling in life than a negative self-image, and it seemed to me that no one in my school system—or in any other school system I knew—was giving much attention to that problem. Every school administrator I have ever met would agree that kids who feel good about themselves perform better, and learn more, but I had never been told how to do anything about it.

For twenty-three years as a classroom teacher, coach, principal, and superintendent, I had seen a parade of new programs designed to improve the quality of public education, but never once had I heard anyone tell educators how to help the student build a positive self-image.

I was desperate to think of a way to move my school system off dead center, to do something that would jolt us out of our cycle of ineffectualness; and as I thought about the root problems of those ten thousand students, I became convinced that the solution lay in changing the way they felt about themselves.

When I trusted that intuition, a process began that, within two years, would produce dramatic improvements in virtually every aspect of our school system. By any yardstick of effective education, District Two would measure substantial gains:

• Grades would improve throughout the system, as would performance on state and national standardized exams.

• Reading scores by elementary students would jump phenomenally, with the number of third graders performing above the national average increasing from 10 percent to 49 percent in one school in a single year.

• Absenteeism would drop sharply.

• Discipline problems would decrease in almost every high school and junior high school in the system.

• Vandalism, such a major problem that in previous years window-glass breakage alone had cost the system $30,000 a year, would become practically nonexistent.

- Participation in extracurricular activities such as band and chorus would increase.
- Suspensions of students would be reduced from 450 per month to 70 per month.
- Drug and alcohol abuse in the secondary schools would decrease.
- Athletic teams would win regional and state championships for the first time in their histories.

If all this sounds little short of miraculous, I should admit that I was as surprised by it as anyone else. It was as if we had turned loose a force in our community that was far more potent than we imagined, and even the most optimistic among us were startled by the results. By creating small improvements in our students' views of themselves, it seemed we received enormous payoffs in their performances.

Charting the progress in the Sumter schools in those next two years was like watching research on the importance of self-esteem leap into life. All those slogans and pep talks became flesh-and-blood reality in rural South Carolina, and being part of it was exciting.

The impact of that experience would do more than just make me a better educator. It would make me a better father and a better husband; it would teach me things about children that I hadn't learned in all my years in graduate school. It would help me to understand why things had worked out as they had in my own personal life, and how my experience could be used to help others.

Sometimes I am tempted to wish that I could retrieve my earlier days as a father, live them over again, knowing what I now know about a child's self-esteem and how to build it. I would be a better father to my two little boys if I had it to do over again, not because I love them more—I loved them then!—or because I would try harder—I was trying my best then!—but because I understand so much better how to be a father of kids who feel good about themselves. The behavioral changes in students, educators, and parents taught me much I wish I had learned long ago.

In that discouraging time in 1978, however, I was unaware of any of the events that would eventually occur. I was just a jaded school administrator trying to solve a problem, and I started the way most executives start on most problems: I pulled a yellow legal pad from a drawer, laid it on top of my desk, and stared at it.

It was time to think about myself. Dr. H. William Mitchell had much in common with these Sumter youngsters, after all. To them I may have been a middle-aged, middle-class, educational "big shot," a successful community leader as unlike themselves as anyone they could imagine. But I knew better. I knew that my background was much more similar to theirs than any of them realized. Lying somewhere just beneath the surface of the Dr. Mitchell they saw was little Billy Mitchell from Alabama. And little Billy Mitchell grew up as poor, as underprivileged, and as afflicted with a sense of inferiority as any kid in Sumter County. Little Billy Mitchell was a runt, always painfully aware of his small size, always defensive about it and ready to fight—and usually lose—to the bigger boys.

Little Billy Mitchell grew up in a steel mill community where nobody went to college, where the challenge was putting food on the table, where lunch at school was leftover biscuits wrapped in yesterday's newspaper. Little Billy Mitchell went to school without shoes, and habitually put his hand over his mouth when he talked, so severe was his fear of saying the wrong thing, of being embarrassed. Little Billy Mitchell thought he wasn't as good as the other kids, and most of them might have agreed with him.

None of the Sumter County students knew it, of course, but little Billy Mitchell was still alive, somewhere beneath the carefully groomed surface of Dr. H. William Mitchell; and when I saw school kids who were crippled by their negative self-images, kids who were convinced that the good life was intended for others, for better people, it broke me up emotionally. My heart went out to them; I knew their pain, because I had been there, and sometimes I wanted to grab those kids physically and hug or shake or do something to them to say, "You are somebody! You are not a nobody! You've got good stuff inside you, and you can bring it out and do great things with it!"

Those Sumter County kids who saw themselves as "have-nots" naturally saw me as a lifelong "have," but I knew better. I knew about little Billy Mitchell with cardboard in his shoes. And for the first time in my life, sitting there staring at that yellow legal pad, I began a systematic attempt to determine what had happened in my own life to bring me from that steel mill town to where I was. If I could isolate the influences that helped me break out of my own vicious cycle of inferiority and negative self-image, it might suggest a place to start in Sumter District Two.

I began to make a list. It soon filled a page, a random list of names and phrases and fragments of memory, each of them representing a time and place in my early life when the notion took hold that I was capable of success and achievement. Out of that hodgepodge of scrawled names and phrases, a pattern emerged. If it is correct that every man's truth is found in his own autobiography, as has been claimed, then it was predictable that I might learn things from reflecting on

my own childhood experiences that I would never find in the professional literature.

As I read over that list of names and places that had been important to my educational life, I literally was so overcome with emotion that I had a physical reaction. It sounds, as I tell it today, a bit weird, but it is true: sweat broke out on the palms of my hands; I felt an adrenaline surge; my heart beat double time. I was forcibly struck by the long list of people who had touched my life, usually with no awareness of the powerful impact they were having. It was obvious that those people, and those events, had taught me something more important than any of my lessons in algebra or biology or English grammar. Informally, instinctively, like so many teachers in so many schools for so many generations, they had taught me that I was a person of worth and value, that they believed in me and my potential.

Until that afternoon, I had never given any particular thought to the patterns of my own development. I had more or less taken for granted what had happened in my life; I knew I was a tough, scrappy kid who had somehow broken out of a very poor background. That day, for the first time, I saw a pattern, a lineup of caring adults who had helped me change my self-image from a nobody to a somebody.

I read over the list a second time, then stared at the words on that yellow pad. I was astonished. It seemed so clear. Spontaneously, I shouted loudly, "Hey, that's it! That's the answer!"

3

When steel mills and smokestacks are mentioned, most people think of Pittsburgh, Cleveland, and the other large cities of the North and Midwest which make up the industrial "Rust Belt." There is a place that is both southern and industrial, a town that many people are surprised to learn is one of the country's major steel producers, and that is Birmingham, Alabama, and the adjacent town of Fairfield. Birmingham and Fairfield may be the only places in the country where the normally contrasting stereotypes of big-city steelworkers and southern rednecks might describe the same group of people.

I grew up in the Birmingham-Fairfield area, in a family whose lives revolved around work in the steel mills. When there was work to be had, it was the heavy labor of the steel mill; and often there was not even enough of that kind of work to go around. Jobs were scarce and pay was low, but work in the mills was the only work we knew. Our family's economic fortune fluctuated between barely having enough and not having anything at all—the condition of our finances at any given time depended on the state of the steel industry. We were poor and so was everyone else we knew. Until I started school in the first grade, I had no way of knowing that, in some homes, there was enough food, clothing, and money to go around.

The only big meals, those with meat on the table, came on the Sunday afternoons when our extended family would gather. The meat was almost always fried chicken, and in the southern custom, we children ate after the adults were finished. They sat down at the table, and we watched while they ate. After their lingering conversation—as well as the choice pieces of chicken—was finished, the table was reset and the children were fed. I was almost grown before I discovered that a chicken has edible parts other than necks, wings, and backs. As a supplement to the usually depleted main course, bread and a big bowl of peanut butter and jelly were placed on the table, and we filled up on that.

I learned to dread those family get-togethers, because I was small for my age, extremely self-conscious about it, and painfully shy. It seemed that every time the cousins were around, we would be stood up back-to-back for the adults to compare our heights and make rather obvious comments about how short and slight I was. In whatever ways the members of the family competed, I came out on the short end.

After the meals, it was our custom to congregate in the living room for music and singing. Those who could play the guitar did; those who could sing jostled for the stage. It seemed to me that everyone had a good time but me. I simply sought a corner and sat and listened, always afraid someone might drag me into the center of the room and reveal my lack of talent and self-confidence.

When I began school, I discovered that being poor

was not necessarily a universal condition, that some people had more of almost everything than some others did. I was aware for the first time that I was from a poor family, from the wrong side of town, and learning this embarrassed me further and heightened my feelings of personal inadequacy. I became sensitized to the small symbols of economic disparity that existed in that school and community. School lunches cost ten cents per day, for example, but there was never any question as to whether I could buy a hot lunch—we simply did not have the dime to spend. I carried my lunch from home—usually leftover biscuits from the breakfast table, occasionally with canned meat or fig preserves inside the biscuit—wrapped in a piece of newspaper.

The socioeconomic caste system of that school was fairly rigidly defined and included the manner in which one's lunch was packaged: the kids from well-fixed families paid ten cents for a hot meal or, if they brought food from home, carried it in lunch buckets. The kids from more modest homes brought their lunches to school in brown paper bags purchased from the local grocer for that purpose. Those of us who were on the bottom of the lunchtime status ladder brought our food wrapped in newspapers. The significance of it was not lost on me, even as a seven- or eight-year-old child. I was embarrassed to eat in the presence of other kids and would often toss my bundle of biscuits into the nearest trash can and spend the lunch period on the school playground.

Mrs. McIndoe was my second-grade teacher and the first adult who intervened to rescue me from the negative self-concept I was already building. Some people might have called her a do-gooder or a bleeding heart; I don't know. All I know is that to a little second grader with cold feet and a large load of hang-ups she was like Florence Nightingale.

Birmingham does not have severe winters, but the weather can get raw and blustery during the cold months. I remember one such morning in particular. It was cold and rainy, and I had to walk just over a mile to school. The only pair of shoes I owned was torn up, worn out, falling apart, so, with the flawed logic of a seven-year-old, I chose not to wear them. We always went barefoot during warm weather. When I got to school that morning, the other children were huddled around the pot-bellied stove that provided heat for the classroom. My feet were freezing, but I entered the classroom and went immediately to my desk and tucked my feet underneath to try to hide them. My humiliation at having no shoes was greater than the pain in my feet.

Mrs. McIndoe saw me. Soon after I arrived, she called the roll and instructed the class to go to the lunchroom to decorate a bulletin board there as a class project. As my classmates rose to file from the room, she placed her hand on my shoulder and said, "Billy, I'd sure appreciate it if you would stay here and help me." Once everyone else was gone, she told me to go over to the stove, put my feet up, and warm them. A little boy never obeyed a teacher's instructions more eagerly!

Mrs. McIndoe called the principal to the room and told me he was going to take me home to get some shoes. "I don't have any," I told him. "The only shoes I have are torn up; the bottoms are knocked out of 'em." He took me home; no one was there. He got my shoes—what was left of them—cut out pieces of cardboard to fit the missing soles, and, with those on my feet, we returned to school. That afternoon, Mrs.

McIndoe and my mother took me to the US Steel commissary and bought new shoes for me on credit.

That experience, if handled differently, could have dealt a further blow to my already tattered self-esteem. The important outcome of the episode, though, was my realization that Mrs. McIndoe cared about me, not just enough to put shoes on my feet, but enough to do so in a way that would protect me from further damage to my ego. Most teachers are observant enough to spot a boy with no shoes on a cold day; Mrs. McIndoe spotted my more serious need for a bolstering of self-confidence. She managed to get shoes on me without confirming to me my label of being just another poverty case. And throughout that school year, she worked at building me up, helping me develop a feeling of self-worth. She interceded at a critical time.

Thank God for sports. So many young boys have used sports to fight their way out of the ghetto, or off the farm, that the athletic route to the middle class has become an American cliché. We all read with pride the stories of the celebrated examples of this pattern, the Floyd Pattersons and the Muhammad Alis, or the Julius Ervings and Herschel Walkers in more recent times. Yet, for every rags-to-riches story of freshly minted athletic millionaires, there are thousands of less spectacular cases in which sports have given inferiority-stricken youngsters a solid sense of self-worth for the first time in their lives. I was one of those cases. I never became a great athlete, but, like most kids, I enjoyed playing almost any kind of sport and had the drive and intensity that made me good at them. Throughout elementary and junior high school, athletics was my lifeboat; playing ball kept me afloat emotionally and psychologically. It gave me something to do that I could do well, and it brought me into contact with adults who built my self-confidence.

Coach Minto was one of those adults. He served double duty as principal and basketball coach at Rutledge Junior High. As a seventh grader there, I was far too shy and self-conscious about my height (an even five feet tall) to try out for the varsity basketball team, but I spent every spare minute on the playground playing in pickup basketball games. It was a plain dirt court, with no nets on the baskets, just the rim and backboard, but the brand of ball played was pretty intense sometimes, and I thrived on its rough-and-tumble style. I was a good shooter, and I never minded diving for loose balls or taking a beating to drive to the basket.

Coach Minto often stayed around the school grounds after hours and on weekends, and although I never paid much attention to him, he noticed me. One day, he singled me out, calling me over to where he was. I wondered which rule I might have broken, but he had entirely something else on his mind. "Billy"— he came right to the point—"I want you to try out for the varsity basketball team."

I was stunned! This had to be a put-on of some kind! Why not say, "Billy, I want you to run for governor of Alabama," or maybe, "Billy, I want you to invent a cure for polio." Better still, why not demand something remotely possible like, "Billy, I want you to swim to Europe." But no, this adult, this coach was telling me he wanted me to try out for the Rutledge Junior High varsity basketball team.

When I overcame my shock to the point where I could speak, I stuttered out my objections: I was too small, anyone could see I was too small; besides which, I had never been on a team before, and all those guys were much better than I, and not only that, but, oh golly, I was much too small! Coach Minto wasn't even listening. He smiled as I went through my fear-stricken monologue, then dismissed the entire argument with a single firm reply: "Nonsense," he said. "Of course you're big enough. Bigness is in the heart, not the body." And that was it. He obviously was not going to let me off the hook so easily.

I made the team. I actually made the team and was assigned a jersey, and when I held that badly worn purple-and-gold jersey number 3 in my hands, I knew beyond any doubt that I would gladly die for the glory of Rutledge Junior High School and the approval of Coach Minto. To me, any coach, for that matter anyone with a college degree, was practically a god, and when this god smiled at me, put a uniform in my hands, told me I could do it, well, of course I would die for him!

Coach Minto was the first person who ever said emphatically to me, "You can do it." He told me not to worry about my lack of height; I was agile, quick, and aggressive, he told me, and I played a strong defensive game. He was confident I could help the team, and his confidence gave birth to my own. My attitude about myself began to change. Maybe I *could* achieve something, if Coach Minto felt that way about it.

The first game in which I played was against Bessemer Junior High. They had an indoor gymnasium, and none of us had ever seen one before. We were awestruck; we could not have been more impressed if we had walked into the White House. It was our first time to play in a gym with a wooden floor and a scoreboard. I was sent into the game that day, scored three points, and played defense like a man possessed. Coach Minto came to me afterward. A man of few words, he congratulated me on my game, paused, looked at me more closely, and said simply, "I told you that you could do it." Nothing profound about that, but those words put a fire in me. I vowed to myself then and there that I would never disappoint Coach Minto. "Please, God, let me die a horrible death before I disappoint Coach Minto." I would pay the price to be a good player, and I would never, ever let this man down.

At the end of the seventh grade, my family moved from our rural home to Elyton Village, an enormous federal housing project in the city of Birmingham. The move was forced by our financial condition; we had no choice. But the prospect of leaving my new friends and teammates, and my Rock of Gibralter, Coach Minto, was unthinkable. We had to do what we had to do, and I understood, so I didn't try to talk my mother out of moving. Instead, I decided to find a way to stay at Rutledge.

It was twenty-five miles from the housing project back to Rutledge Junior High, which could be reached only by taking a commercial bus to the town of Fairfield, then transferring to another bus to Rutledge. My mother was working in a defense plant and couldn't afford the extra cost of that daily transportation for me, but she agreed to let me try it if I could earn the money myself. So I made the commitment to pay my own way—anything to stay in the positive, accepting environment I had found under Coach Minto. I looked for odd jobs, and I found them, some of them very odd jobs indeed!

My first job came from the housing project director. The project had a major rat problem, and the director offered me and several other boys a job hunting and killing rats. The pay was one cent for every six dead rats we could deliver to him; it may have been the most cost-effective pest-control program on record. Arming ourselves with clubs, we set out to earn those pennies. It took a bit of skill and a lot of speed. One of our favorite tactics was to shake the incinerators to force the rats out into the open where we could get a whack at them.

There were other, less exotic ways to earn busfare, such as mowing lawns and cleaning debris off construction sites. I also worked as a skate boy at a roller rink, helping fit skates on the customers; as a curb boy at the local ice-cream parlor; and at other temporary jobs here and there. Somehow, I always came up with enough money for busfare and lunches to be able to stay at Rutledge.

I left home at 6:30 each morning, rode those two buses to school, and felt great about myself all the way. That year, not surprisingly, my rapidly growing self-confidence began to affect my academic performance. For the first time ever, I made good grades. I started to take an interest in my dress and grooming. The belief in me that Coach Minto expressed was having a domino effect; it was spreading to other areas of my life, and as I ventured more, and succeeded more, I believed in myself more.

Living conditions in the projects, which can sometimes be so damaging to the development of boys like myself, had little impact on me. I was so caught up in my involvement at school, so under the influence of Coach Minto and his positive attention, that I barely noticed what was going on around me in the housing projects. The peer group that mattered to me was at Rutledge; the adult model who mattered to me was there; and the negative influences so often encountered by kids growing up in the projects never had a chance to operate in my case.

* * *

4

ngels are packaged in various ways, and at West End High School my nurturing angel came in the form of an ROTC sergeant.

West End High was one of Birmingham's largest schools, its fourteen hundred students coming from many different neighborhoods that cut across the city's social strata. Most of the kids were from middle-income homes, and those of us who commuted the several miles by streetcar from the federal housing projects were clearly identified as the West End's lowest caste. We were from the wrong side of the tracks, we were excluded from the trendy activities and groups, and we were probably scratchy and hostile as a result. The teachers generally expected us to have very little potential and to be the source of most of their discipline problems. So we didn't disappoint them.

I got off to a bad start at West End. With no Coach Minto to prop me up, and no way to transfer my Rutledge reputation to this cold and forbidding place, I sought attention in the way most of my friends did—by causing trouble.

Fortunately, there was at least one West End faculty member who gave me a chance to earn some respect. Sergeant Lacey, head of the Army ROTC unit at West End, apparently saw in me something other than the "tuffies" I wore (those were the durable factory-worker's pants that marked me as a lower-class kid), the underdeveloped vocabulary, and the awkward social skills, and saw whatever Mrs. McIndoe and Coach Minto had seen. He took an interest in me, and I always knew it was genuine.

Sergeant Lacey made a boxer out of me. He helped train kids for the Golden Gloves competition in Birmingham, and persuaded me to learn to box and enter the local tournament. Sergeant Lacey was not coy about my background; he was not reluctant to use the word *poor*. He was straightforward in talking to me about myself—no euphemisms or verbal dodging with him. He talked to me continuously about other people who had overcome poverty; he told stories of great men and women in history who had started with nothing; he addressed directly and specifically my need to overcome the sense of inferiority that was so apparent.

I entered the Golden Gloves, won many matches, and eventually won the Birmingham championship in my weight division. I got lots of local publicity and suddenly found myself a person recognizable to my peers in high school. But, more importantly, I experienced once again the feeling of wanting to live up to someone's expectations, and doing so. Sergeant Lacey believed in me, and I measured up! That was a bigger payoff to me than receiving a trophy or getting my name in the paper. I began to drop by his office, whenever I had a chance, just to talk with him, and he always had time to chat. I basked in his belief in me.

Sergeant Lacey's influence reached into another area, my social life, which up to that time had been nonexistent. Soon after I won the Golden Gloves tournament, he challenged me to get a date to the upcoming ROTC ball. I had the usual excuses: no car, no driver's license even if I had a car, never had a date before, didn't know how to dance anyway—all very logical reasons, none of which impressed Sergeant Lacey. "No problem," he said. He would teach me to drive, he would lend me his car, he would see that I learned how to dance, and as for not having a date before, well, there was always a first time for everything.

The only thing I had to do for myself was to ask a girl.

Sergeant Lacey left me little room to argue, so we went to work. I learned to drive, got my license, and learned an awkward version of the jitterbug. I was paralyzed by the thought of asking a girl for a date, but by then I had some momentum, and I figured I may as well ask a pretty one. I did, and she said okay. It all happened very fast.

When the big night came, I dressed up in my ROTC uniform (I had never owned a suit or sport coat at that time), got behind the wheel of a borrowed Hudson, and felt ten feet tall—for me, the ultimate euphoria!

The anxieties of learning to drive, asking a girl for a date, of going to my first dress-up ball, all of it was too much for me. By the time the dance had begun, I was feeling nauseated and then desperately sick. I stumbled through one slow dance, then bluffed my way through a jitterbug ("Woodchopper's Ball"), and was too sick to go any further. I took the girl home then and there and sneaked back into the housing project only a couple of hours after I had left, a little embarrassed but too nauseated to care.

To the girl who had unwittingly shared this virginal

occasion with me, the evening was no doubt an unmitigated failure, but even its abrupt and ignominious conclusion could not diminish my sense of accomplishment. To me, having a dress-up date was a major breakthrough, and just having survived it represented a monumental achievement.

I find it difficult to believe, looking back, that for eighteen years of my life I had never considered the possibility of going to college. To graduate from high school would be to reach an educational level neither of my parents had attained; I considered a high school graduate to be a well-educated person and regarded the goal of entering college as boldly ambitious. The idea that I might go to college never occurred to me until my first year in the Army.

My mother's and stepfather's families were all steel mill workers; that was all any of us knew. Conversation in our home was always talk of unions, seniority, and overtime. "Making it" to me had always meant getting a secure job in a local steel mill. Formal education was regarded as something for that more sophisticated breed of people who lived on the other side of town. So when I set my sights on getting a high school diploma, I regarded it as a fairly audacious goal in itself and ignored the idea of college—it was a luxury for rich intellectuals. When I graduated from high school, I intended to go into the Army to fulfill my service obligation, and from there to the mills.

Sometime between that first Lacey-inspired dance date and my high school graduation, I fell in love! Nothing especially unusual about that—high school boys fall in love all the time, some of them as often as once or twice a week. But, as it turned out, this really *was* love. Her name was Carolyn. I first saw her in the school library, wearing a pink blouse and a corduroy skirt, reading a book, looking for all the world like Venus to my young and eager eyes. I asked the librarian for her name, went to the school office and got her home phone number, and talked myself into calling her to ask for a date. She said no. The conversation was very brief.

I thought I knew what the problem was: she was from a well-fixed family on the more fashionable side of town. I wasn't good enough for her. It was an indication of my growing self-confidence that I pursued her anyway; I went to the library more often in the next two weeks than in the previous two years. She was always there, and I tried to make conversation with her. She was aloof and disinterested. Becoming more and more discouraged, I talked with Sergeant Lacey about it. "Don't give up on her," he challenged me. "Just hang in there. She'll come around."

I did, and she did. This is the kind of story that can become very long and complicated, but the end of it all is that Carolyn did eventually agree to date me, despite the enormous differences in the social status of our families. Soon we became close friends and, in a short time, were, in the lingo of our generation, "going steady." Visiting her in her home reminded me of how totally different our environments were, but rather than being intimidated by that, I found somewhat to my surprise that I was motivated to earn my place in that world which she had always known and taken for granted.

My senior year was almost over, and I had signed induction papers to enter the United States Army on the morning after my high school graduation. I wanted to ask Carolyn to wait for me, to promise to marry me when I returned from my military hitch, but fear of being rejected made me delay asking until the latest possible moment. The West End High graduation exercises were on a Friday night, and I was to leave late that same night for Fort Jackson, South Carolina, to be inducted into active duty.

Carolyn went to see me graduate, and after the ceremony was over, the two of us went to the top of Red Mountain to say our good-byes. Red Mountain is a favorite attraction in Birmingham, especially for romantic types. There is a gigantic statue of Vulcan, the Iron Man, holding his lamp high above the city; inside are steps that lead to the top. At night, young couples climb Red Mountain to look down on the city lights, twinkling and glowing with their distant colors. There, with that movie-set backdrop, rushing to beat the midnight curfew her parents strictly enforced, I finally persuaded Carolyn to wait for me and to marry me when my military tour was completed. She was as good as her promise, and we are as much in love today as we were that night on Red Mountain.

After she said yes, I got her home by midnight, and five hours later boarded a train for Fort Jackson.

5

I spent most of my two years in the Army doing what most recruits do—looking forward to becoming a civilian again.

To me, serving in the military was something I owed my country, so I did my time as cheerfully and constructively as possible, but my heart was always back home in Birmingham. I boxed while in the service and was as successful as I had been in high school, winning the Fifth Army championship and later serving as a boxing instructor in the Special Services division at Camp Attenbury, Indiana.

But most of all I worked. I was never a gung-ho soldier type, but I was conscientious about my Army life, and by now my drive to excel in whatever I did was gaining momentum. By the time I got to Fort Benning, Georgia, I was well on my way to becoming a high achiever. The Army can be a great social leveler; the symbols of clothing and life-style that label some young men as poor and others as middle class or wealthy are largely absent in the life of an enlisted man, and for the first time I found myself able to interact with other people without feeling like a poor kid from the wrong side of the tracks. It was a liberating experience, as it has been to so many people from disadvantaged backgrounds, to wear a military uniform and be free of the most obvious trappings of one's social class. I found that I was in almost every respect "as good as the best, and better than the rest," as the old line goes.

I never cashed any of my Army checks. I sent every nickel home to my family, to be saved for the day of my discharge. I was determined to have a nest egg put aside for Carolyn and me when our time came to start married life. I made extra money working at the box office of the post theater and by pulling extra shifts for soldiers who wanted to get away for a few hours. Other small jobs could be found around the base, and I never missed a chance to make a few dollars for spending money, so my Army paychecks could go home untouched. The word wasn't in vogue at the time, but I was something of a workaholic, so appealing was the goal I was working toward.

On the occasions when I had a few days' leave, I hitched a ride back to Birmingham, straight to Carolyn's house, pitched my duffel bag on her porch with a certain military flourish to announce my arrival, and stayed right there until it was time to return to base.

After two years in the service, I was honorably discharged and headed home, all of twenty years old, to cash in my nest egg, marry my girl, and begin a new life.

I arrived in Birmingham and immediately the roof fell in.

When I arrived to collect that pot of money I had been saving for those two years, there was no money to collect. It was gone. All of it. Vanished. My shock and disbelief made me almost physically ill. My family had experienced serious problems, they explained; my mother had been unable to work, and the money I had sent home had been used to keep things together. My joy at finally being out of the service evaporated immediately. All that time I had barely existed on bits and pieces of income in order to save for marriage; I hadn't even bought any civilian clothes. I was devastated.

Nothing to do but start over; Carolyn and I would have to delay our wedding plans until I had saved some money. After the anger had passed and the depression lifted a bit, I started looking for a job to rebuild the kitty. Carolyn's father lent me enough money to buy some clothes, and I found a job at Tennessee Coal and Iron, a local subsidiary of US Steel. I shared a cheap apartment with a young man and started to work.

I was a steelworker at last. The tentative, vague idea of perhaps going to college, that seed planted at West End High School and nourished by my successes in the Army, would stay dormant for a while longer. At the time, I thought the notion was dead entirely.

When I finally became a steelworker—the thing I always assumed would be the top of the ladder for me—I found I was a total misfit. The world of the steel mill and the union hall was the world I had grown up in, the only world my family knew, and rather than feeling at home, I found, to my surprise, that I was restless and frustrated there.

The people who worked at Tennessee Coal and Iron were good people, salt-of-the-earth people, but they were limited in their interests. All the talk at TCI was of layoffs, shop slowdowns, pay scales, and benefits, and the only goals seemed to be to survive until quitting time each day and payday each week. This had seemed perfectly normal to me a few years earlier, but since I had begun dreaming of better things, it depressed me. I fought the unhappiness by working as many hours as possible, and thinking about better days.

I worked as an electrician's helper wherever there was an electrical problem anywhere in the plant. I knew most of the men, learned who enjoyed fishing and hunting, and let them know I was always available to work their shifts when they wanted to take off a day. I got lots of overtime that way, working almost every holiday for men who wanted to be with their families.

Working in a steel mill is hot and dangerous work. The heavy steel-toed shoes and protective headgear are cumbersome. The jobs are usually monotonous and physically demanding. I didn't mind hard work, but I began to wonder if forty-five years of this was really what I wanted from life. I envied the supervisors who came through the plant and the way my fellow mill workers looked up to them. We did the routine tasks, and what the supervisors were doing seemed more interesting work. But when I asked about what it took to be a supervisor, someone told me that the best jobs at that level were reserved for people with college degrees. Maybe that was when the seed began to grow again.

Carolyn worked in an office at a factory twenty miles away. We hoarded almost everything we made, pooled our funds, and within a year had enough to get married. It was a simple home wedding. No frills. And no honeymoon; we spent the night in our new one-bedroom apartment and both went back to work the next morning.

After I became a married man, the hunger for a better life grew sharply, and I decided to find out what kind of shot I might have at college. My strategy was to make all the preliminary inquiries without telling

Carolyn. If things looked impossible, I was determined she would never know I was unhappy in the steel mill. I checked into the GI Bill and found I was entitled to $150 per month if I went to college. I looked for a part-time job and was promised a coaching job at the local YMCA. With that paycheck and the GI Bill, I thought we could get by.

So I told Carolyn. She was flabbergasted. She knew how eager I had been to get out of high school, knew that I never had made plans to go to college, and that my high school academic record was very poor. And there was the gamble of giving up the security of a full-time job to go to college. It all sounded pretty ridiculous as we talked about it, but she was willing to take the risk.

Then I talked to admissions counselors at the two local colleges, Howard (now Samford University) and Birmingham Southern. The first person I talked with at Birmingham Southern put my chances into perspective for me. Pointing out that nothing in my high school transcript indicated any aptitude for college work, he suggested that if I didn't like the steel mill, perhaps I should try to get a job that did not require a college education. That was not what I wanted to hear.

Fortunately, I was assigned to another counselor, this one a coach, and he had a different opinion entirely. He had hardly any interest at all in my high school grades, focusing instead on the other parts of my record, and before the day was over, he had secured for me admission to Birmingham Southern and even found me a spot in the married students' apartment complex. All I had to do was make passing grades for the first academic term, and I would be fully admitted.

I gave the supervisor at the mill my notice, moved with Carolyn to the campus apartments, and the Rubicon was crossed. Whenever I stopped to think about the chance we were taking, it scared me to death. I studied every waking moment that first term. Nothing came easily. In my low moments, I kicked myself for making such a reckless move, with so much depending on those first grades. I knew my first set of grades would be the acid test for me. I knew that to fail now would mean a lifetime in the steel mill, and that dismal prospect kept me going.

Of course, I made it. When the first term ended, my grades were not great, but they were good enough. I was in to stay, a full-time college freshman at the age of twenty-three. I finished the four-year liberal arts program in two years and ten months, graduating with a bachelor of arts degree in physical education.

6

When I entered college, my goals were still so thoroughly dominated by life in a steel mill community that I thought of college primarily as a way of getting a better job in the mill.

A college degree was, at first, simply a way to escape the drudgery of the production line for the more interesting work and better pay of a supervisor. My horizons were still limited by a mill-town mentality. And, sure enough, when I graduated in 1957, US Steel offered me a management job at what was then an excellent salary of six thousand dollars a year.

But sometime during those two years and ten months of college, my perspective had changed. As my own self-esteem had improved, I had come to think less in terms of merely surviving, merely making a living, and had come to understand more and more that the best payoffs in life are the intangible ones. Somewhere along the way my goals had evolved. I began to think of making a contribution, of giving back to the system some of the emotional support others had given to me. I began to think about a career in education.

Upon graduation, another job offer came my way, this one from my old alma mater, West End High School. It paid little more than half what I was offered at US Steel. The choice was as clear as one could have, and it was hardly a decision at all: I rejected the steel company job and signed up to teach and coach at West End High.

Looking back on that watershed decision, I realize that I took the teaching job not because of an overwhelming altruistic urge or because I felt like doing the noble thing. It was the natural thing for me to do, and was accompanied by no great sense of sacrifice or bleeding-heart missionary zeal. My choice was a testimony to the educators in my life who had made me what I was; I wanted to become an educator myself. My case is one of hundreds of thousands of such examples of the self-sustaining nature of the educational process, whenever sensitive and caring teachers intervene in the lives of students as they had in mine.

It was the teachers in my life—not the doctors or the politicians or the businessmen—who had given me a sense of self-worth, and consequently, it was the teachers whom I had come to emulate, and their profession that I valued and wished to join. By the time the decision came, it was virtually already made for me; I turned to education as naturally as cows head for the barn at milking time.

My relatives, of course, thought I was crazy.

I was still small and looked young, I suppose. It felt strange to walk the halls of West End High as a teacher rather than student, and apparently some of my faculty colleagues had as much trouble with the transition as I did. One day during the first week of school, I was standing in the hall talking to some of my athletes. A teacher stepped out of her classroom and asked each of us for his name. We were talking too loudly, it seems, and she was reporting us for a disciplinary infraction. When she got to me, I simply answered "Billy Mitchell." She gave each of us a demerit slip and sent us to the principal's office for punishment. Rather than embarrass her, I quietly went with the rest of the boys, and I don't think she ever realized I was a fellow teacher.

That year began a career in public education that continues to the present. I taught and coached at West End for nine years, and returned to college to earn a master's degree during that time. I left West End to take a position as principal of an elementary school in Birmingham, and from there moved to Huntsville, Alabama, to serve as principal of Whitesburg Junior High School, one of the largest in the state, with fourteen hundred students.

After that, I returned to school again, this time to the University of Alabama to earn an Ed.D. degree in school administration, teaching in the graduate school of education while I was at the university. From there I moved one last step up the educational career ladder, accepting a job as superintendent of city schools in Athens, Alabama. A superintendency in Dillon, South Carolina, followed, and finally, the challenges of District Two in Sumter.

It is a long road from the steel mills to Sumter County District Two, but it is a story of the transformation of a person's attitude about himself and is a story that has been repeated many times in this country. In nearly every case, the same three elements affect the storyline:

• The development of a positive self-image as a child was essential for any eventual success as an adult.

• The self-image development occurred largely as a result of the intervention of caring adults.

• Those adults were usually a part of the school system.

The more I stared at my yellow legal pad that day in my Sumter office, reading over and over names like McIndoe, Minto, Lacey, and many others, the more strongly I felt that the answers to District Two's problems of low student achievement lay there.

If my case were an isolated one, or if I were exceptionally talented or bright, there would perhaps be little to learn from my story. But I was not a gifted child in any sense. The happy ending in my life story was a result of the three principles stated above: *key people in the public schools intuitively did the things that made me feel good about myself, and my behavior gradually shaped itself to match that self-image.*

I thought of all the stories I had read of great achievers and leaders throughout history, and the pattern holds. The problem is that the process is too random, the misses are more frequent than the hits. The number of kids lucky enough to have teachers like mine is overwhelmed by the kids who go through the school system without ever meeting an adult who seeks to teach them how to feel good about themselves.

We need a systematic program designed to improve the way students feel about themselves, to broaden their attitudes about their own limits and potentials. It is simply not good enough to hope that the students in our schools will be lucky enough to encounter a teacher who will say and do the right things instinctively to change their students' negative mind-sets.

Our challenge in Sumter District Two was to implement a program to build the self-esteem of our students, a 185-day program that would encourage, uplift, and positively reinforce our kids every day.

That was clearly a big order, but I was convinced we had to attempt it. More money is spent on education today than at any time in our history, yet the results are less and less satisfactory. We have tried almost everything except the one solution that holds the greatest promise—the development of the self-image of learners. It is essential that schools work as hard to develop feelings of self-worth and self-confidence among their students as they work to develop basic skills. Albert Einstein once said, "Education is that which remains after you have forgotten everything you learned in school." Education is not collecting a mass of facts; it is acquiring an attitude, a frame of mind, a view of oneself and the world in which one lives.

Another thought bothered me: for almost twenty-five years in education, I had been aware of the relationship between positive attitudes and successful performance, yet I could not think of a single school program that had attempted to teach these important qualities systematically as a part of the instructional program. Sumter District Two, the school system for which I had personal responsibility, did not budget a single penny for the development of self-confidence and positive thinking in its students.

I was determined we were going to change that.

7

A few days after I had listed the people who had changed my life, another event occurred that, though it seemed insignificant and unrelated, had an important influence on what transpired in Sumter District Two.

I was sifting through the mail on my desk one morning, setting aside the junk mail that inevitably pours into a superintendent's office. As I started to dump a batch of it into the wastepaper basket, I noticed a flyer advertising a positive thinking rally to be held in Chicago a few days later. Impulsively, I fished the brochure from the heap and took a closer look.

It was the kind of announcement I had seen many times before—such flyers cross my desk routinely—but it had never occurred to me to consider seriously going to one of the events described. In the first place, Chicago is a long way from Sumter County. Busy administrators do not spend time running halfway across the country to meetings they are not absolutely required to attend. And even if I had the time and money to go to Chicago, what purpose would it serve? From what I had heard, these rallies were more designed for salespeople than for school superintendents; apparently the programs were oriented toward getting people excited about making more money. That had nothing to do with me.

But for some reason the announcement stayed on top of my desk, and the idea of going to that Chicago rally began to grow on me. I read the names of the featured speakers. They were names that I knew: Norman Vincent Peale, Paul Harvey, W. Clement Stone, all of them authors of books that at one time or another I had read.

In my early days of coaching and teaching, I had been a zealous advocate and disciple of the Positive Mental Attitude (PMA) approach to personal achievement. I first had encountered positive thinking ideas in 1957, my first year as a coach, when I was given a copy of what has become a classic, *The Power of Positive Thinking,* by Norman Vincent Peale. I was not much of a reader at that time; I doubt I had ever read more than a dozen books that were not a part of my classroom assignments. But that book made such good sense to me, its arguments were so compelling, that as soon as I had finished reading it once, I started at the beginning and read it straight through again.

Dr. Peale's book and its ideas became a part of my life. I found myself quoting and paraphrasing it to my wife, my students, my athletes, my friends, my two sons. It was as if I had injected it into my blood, so thoroughly did I assimilate its viewpoint. In ten years of coaching, no other single influence was more important to my philosophy of competing and winning than that book.

From Dr. Peale's book, I had gone on to others: *Heart of a Champion,* by Bob Richards, the Olympic pole-vaulting champion; *Laws of Success,* by Sterling

W. Sill; and many others. The concepts in these books were powerful ones, and they were so readily applied to coaching and athletic achievement that I seldom stopped talking about the need for a positive mental attitude during the early years of my career.

By the time I reached Sumter District Two, though, my PMA days seemed part of a distant and rather naive past. As my approach to education became more sophisticated, and the problems of administering school systems demanded so much attention, I had drifted away from the use of those concepts in my work and had stopped reading books on attitude and motivation. I was something of a failed positive thinker, partly because I was too busy and partly because I considered myself somewhat beyond that simplistic sort of approach.

Now, here was this flyer on my desk, with all those old, familiar names. And here I was stuck in a professional rut, looking for solutions they hadn't taught me in graduate school. And here was this yellow legal pad with scribbled names and places that all spoke of the power of self-esteem and positive attitude.

I decided to go to Chicago.

Later that day, a school board member who was a friend of mine came by the office, and I surprised both of us by suggesting that he rearrange his weekend plans and fly with me to Chicago. The very next afternoon, we were on a plane and, shortly afterward, sitting in a large auditorium with several thousand other people, listening to hour after hour of speeches from the men whose names were on the brochure.

As I listened to these men speak with such conviction about the power of positive expectations, then went back home and began to read the motivational books I had bought, it was like meeting an old and valued friend whom I had not seen in a long time. I felt that the problems and needs of the children in Sumter District Two were coming into focus. The missing ingredient was one of attitude; we needed a wall-to-wall program for building positive attitudes, starting with our teachers and school staff, including parents, and spreading inevitably to the students themselves.

I looked around at other members of that Chicago audience and saw that the crowd was mostly business-people, sales and management types. These were the people who had most readily embraced the concepts of positive thinking, and as a result, the PMA viewpoint had become associated with making money and achieving success in the business and corporate world. But why should that be? I asked myself. Why should the people with material and financial goals be more aware of PMA concepts, and more willing to utilize them, than those of us in public education?

In his speech that day, Clement Stone made one statement that particularly struck home: "Only one percent of the people who apply the principles of positive thinking in their lives acquired this philosophy from the schools." *What a waste!* I thought.

If the principles of positive mental attitude are valid, would they not work just as well for the schoolteacher as for the salesperson? If these mental techniques can help a corporate manager develop happier and more productive employees, can't they help a principal run a more effective elementary, middle, or high school? If these concepts are basic to human nature, I reasoned, shouldn't we public educators lead the parade in applying them to the needs of our students?

Of course we should! Why let the business world have a corner on such powerful concepts, while we in public education overlook them?

Napoleon Hill made the case very well:

One of the irreparable losses to the human race lies in the lack of knowledge that there is a definite method through which self-confidence can be developed in any person of average intelligence. What a loss that young men and women are not taught this known method of developing self-confidence before they complete their schooling, for no one who lacks faith in himself is really educated in the proper sense of the term.

Okay, Mr. Hill, I thought, *you're right. And in at least one place in this country, in Sumter County District Two, we are going to do something about it!*

8

The program of positive thinking and self-esteem development that we began in Sumter District Two produced dramatic improvements in the effectiveness of our schools and eventually became the basis for a national foundation that is presently bringing the program to other school systems across the country.

The secrets of that program are not limited to the classroom alone, however. The program is a set of techniques for anyone who wants to help a child or teen-ager get more from life. Most parents are eager to help their children do well in school, in sports, and other activities—many parents are, in fact, so eager to help that their interaction with the child becomes a daily battle, a tug-of-war in which the conscientious parent tries to inspire or demand better performance from a child who seems determined not to cooperate.

It is common for parents to feel that they want success for the child more than the child wants it for himself. The effort to prod, poke, wheedle, coerce, nag, threaten, bribe, bargain, persuade, or otherwise motivate the child to work harder in school and at home can become a tough challenge for parents. Most of us with school-age children would agree that it is the most difficult parental task we face, and a major source of discouragement for us as parents. The child's unfinished homework, or neglected piano practice, or chronically poor report cards are grounds for battle in many homes. "Never try to teach a pig to sing," a wise man once said. "It will only frustrate you, and annoy the pig." Parents often feel that all their efforts finally result in frustrating themselves and annoying the child!

The principles of building self-esteem can be of enormous value to the millions of parents who find themselves in this situation. As a teacher and principal, I often was asked, "What can I do to help my child get the most from school?" Responsible parents see themselves as partners with the school in producing an effective future adult, and the best job is obviously done when the child is getting the same signals, living in the same emotional climate, seeing displayed the same attitudes, both at home and in school.

To do the job thoroughly, then, we must not only develop positive schools but positive homes as well. The self-esteem training in which the teacher engages must be matched at home by positive parenting—a conscious, ongoing attempt by parents to deal with a child in a way that builds his sense of self-worth.

The fundamental principles that we accepted in Sumter County are these:

• A child's sense of self-worth is highly related to his achievement in school and other areas.

• Positive self-esteem can be taught.

• The responsibility for teaching it lies with both parents and educators, both at home and in school.

These three principles are supported by reams of psychological and educational research. William Purkey, an educational psychologist at the University of North Carolina–Greensboro, is perhaps the most lucid spokesman for the importance of self-esteem in the child's achievement:

> For generations, wise teachers have sensed the significant and positive relationship between a student's concept of himself and his performance in school. They believed that the students who feel good about themselves and their abilities are the ones who are most likely to succeed.

There is no denying that teachers are a major source of the self-concepts of their students. Obviously, much of how the child feels about himself is a direct result of his contacts with parents and teachers; the only question is whether their influence will be positive or negative.

Unfortunately, schooling as we know it today is largely a negative experience for many students. As Dr. Purkey observed, "For too many students, the school is a high risk neighborhood." It has been estimated that during twelve years of schooling, a single child will be bombarded with as many as fifteen thousand *no*'s, *don't*'s, and *can't*'s. Add to these the many hundreds of negative communications they hear in the home and from significant adults elsewhere. The overall picture is of a childhood dominated by warnings and statements that emphasize life's downside risks more than its upside potential. Perhaps we should not find surprising the research report that although 80 percent of children entering school have positive self-images, only about 20 percent still do by the fifth grade, and only about 5 percent feel good about themselves by the time they are high school seniors.

We cannot continue to design programs of instruction and impose them upon our children as if their self-concepts had little bearing on their success or failure as students and human beings. Art Combs, professor emeritus at the University of Florida and a distinguished educator, once commented, "For us to say, 'I know self-concept is important, but I don't have time to deal with that in my classroom,' is about as stupid as saying, 'I know my car needs a carburetor, but I'm going to run mine without one.' Attitude is an inseparable part of the learning process, and it can be taught as surely as mathematics and history."

A child in school who perceives himself as an able learner will behave in the way able learners behave; if he sees himself as a poor learner, he will also behave in a way which verifies that self-perception. If schools are to increase effective performance by their students, the total environment must be modified to sustain the positive feelings most children have about themselves when they enter school.

Once formed, the self-concept is very difficult to change. The child's self-concept becomes a screening device through which all experiences are filtered. A child who thinks of himself as a "loser" will selectively magnify and emphasize those experiences in his life that are consistent with that view, and likewise with the child whose self-view is positive. The result is that the child learns increasingly to make implicit predictions about his own success, and these "prophecies" always tend to be self-fulfilling.

The cycle of self-fulfilling prophecy grows more deeply entrenched each year, unless something intervenes to disrupt the process. Johnny senses that

Daddy expects him to do poorly, and like a sponge absorbs that view of himself. Now Johnny too expects that he will do poorly, and that negative expectation causes him indeed to *do* poorly, which in turn deepens both Daddy's and Johnny's attitude that Johnny is deficient.

According to Dr. Purkey, "Most research findings support the view that students are more than likely to perform as their teachers think they will." Children form images of themselves by their perception of adults' reactions to their behavior, through expressions of approval or disapproval, and these adults all too frequently have expectations for performance that are far below the child's potential.

In a famous experiment conducted by Robert Rosenthal, a developmental psychologist at Harvard University, this tendency of adult expectations to influence the child's performance was graphically demonstrated. In Rosenthal's experiment, a group of students were randomly selected from a class and identified to their teacher as "exceptional" children who could be expected to do above-average work. They were, in fact, no different from the rest of the students in the class, but because the teacher expected them to do well, and interacted with them as if they were superior students, they responded to that expectation by performing at a significantly higher level than the other students.

Positive self-concepts are important not only in the classroom but in the many social skills that the child must master to function well. Discipline in both school and at home is an area directly affected by the child's sense of self-worth. Pressures toward drug and alcohol abuse, skipping classes, disrespect of authority in its various forms, vandalism, shoplifting, and other types of juvenile misbehavior are best resisted by the child with high self-esteem. Children with strong self-concepts also seem less likely to engage in impulsive acting out of inappropriate behaviors. As a general rule, says psychologist T. H. Szasz, "The more self-esteem a person has, the greater is his desire, and his ability, to control himself."

Why have so many educators overlooked, or even actively resisted, an emphasis in the schools on the development of the child's sense of his own worth? With so much available evidence showing its importance, why has the building of positive attitudes not been made a part of the public school curriculum on a widespread basis?

I am convinced that most administrators regard such an emphasis as a "softheaded" approach to education, one that neglects the basic skills of readin', 'ritin', and 'rithmetic. The public is burned out on what it regards as experiments that have not worked—attempts to *substitute* such things as self-awareness and creative expression for the teaching of fundamental skills. There is a demand for basics—that schools teach kids to learn a rudimentary body of knowledge rather than dabbling in pseudopsychological self-expression.

I emphatically agree. The fundamentals must come first. A child who is not learning basic academic skills is failing to achieve the primary purposes of his education, but the development of a healthy self-esteem does not compete with that goal—to the contrary, it greatly facilitates it. A child who feels good about himself learns the multiplication tables more readily than the child who does not. The teaching of self-esteem and the teaching of academic skills are not an either-or process. One enhances the other.

The teacher, or the parent, who takes the time to

teach a child that he is a somebody, and not a nobody, will ultimately need to spend less time teaching that same child how to conjugate a French verb. By building the child's self-esteem, we create a more efficient learning machine, and all the skills we wish to teach him will then come more easily.

It makes good practical sense to spend time on the child's attitude for two reasons: first, as an end in itself, to make a happier child, and second, because the self-confident child will learn everything else more readily.

When we take the time to teach kids to like themselves, we get the best of both worlds.

9

No amount of educational theory would mean very much, of course, unless we could make it work in Sumter County.

How is self-esteem learned? We settled on a simple formula that fits the school and the home equally well. Self-esteem is learned by means of three experiences: *conditioning, modeling,* and *positive reinforcement.* An effective school, like a positive home, must be arranged so that all three of these constantly occurring experiences contribute to the child's positive feelings about himself rather than to his negative feelings about himself.

Every child is being shaped every day by conditioning, modeling, and reinforcement. The question is not whether these three experiences will exist in his environment, but whether they will be of such a nature as to produce high self-esteem.

When the word *conditioning* is used, one immediately thinks of Pavlov's dogs, or perhaps of dark tales of brainwashing and mind-control techniques. Actually, conditioning is the most basic form of learning, and psychologists have studied it for over a hundred years—going back, indeed, to those famous experiments of Ivan Pavlov in which dogs were conditioned to salivate when they heard the sound of a ringing bell. But there is nothing sinister about conditioning; it is merely a term that describes the most powerful and fundamental type of learning.

The thing that distinguishes conditioning from other types of learning is that it can occur without the voluntary participation, or even the knowledge, of the person being conditioned. Learning to change the oil in your car only happens when you set out to learn it; it doesn't happen accidentally, without your being aware of it. Learning most things, like the Greek alphabet or the recipe for homemade fudge sauce or how to play PacMan, requires an intent to learn, or at least an awareness that the learning is occurring. Learning to quote Shakespeare is not the sort of thing that sneaks up on you.

Conditioning, on the other hand, usually *does* sneak up on you. An individual learns something through conditioning without any intent to learn at all. It is almost as if conditioning is something that happens *to* him rather than through his efforts. Fragments of information pour into the brain through the five senses and fuse together through repetition. The process is so basic, so primitive, that it is occurring during every waking moment in the life of every individual. (Experimental studies have shown, in fact, that the phenomenon is so powerful that it occurs with animals that have been anesthetized, and with unborn fetuses in the womb of a human mother.)

Conditioning goes on all the time, saturating us with feelings that become a natural part of the way we respond to everything around us. Most of the elements of one's personal style that seem natural, so natural that he thinks of them as his innate personality, actually are the results of conditioning in early childhood. Things learned through conditioning are not easily lost; they are carved so deeply into our experience that they usually remain there permanently.

Repetition is the key to conditioning. What one hears repeatedly, what one sees constantly, the tone and texture of the external environment of which one is habitually a part, become internalized into the personality of the person himself. It becomes a part of who he is. Different psychologists use different language to describe the process; some talk of programming the mind; some use words like *subconscious mind* and speak of the subconscious absorbing of certain messages and ideas; others talk of *subliminal persuasion.*

Whatever the vocabulary used, the concept is the same: if the mind is bombarded often enough with a message, it eventually is accepted. We were determined in Sumter District Two to use every available means to saturate the consciousness—and even the subconsciousness—of our youngsters with the message that they are people of worth and value. We would use billboards, milk cartons, bulletin boards, school supplies, vehicles, book covers, newsletters, radio and TV ads, pep rallies, special calendars, lapel buttons, and many other ways to hammer home the message. We wanted our students, and our teachers and parents as well, virtually to wallow in a sea of positive communication.

If feelings are learned through conditioning, and conditioning occurs through repetition, then we were determined to have a community in which kids literally could not escape being told, over and over, that they were somebody special.

*   *   *

Modeling is another powerful learning tool that operates in the development of a positive self-image. Modeling is very similar to imitation—in fact, it was originally called "imitative modeling" by the psychologists who first studied this process.

Imitation is a conscious process by which a person intentionally copies another person's behavior. Modeling, on the other hand, takes place unconsciously. It is the process in which one individual gradually takes on the characteristics of someone else, especially someone whom he likes or admires. Modeling is one of the most common types of learning among young children; much of the growing child's everyday learning occurs as he quite naturally picks up the behavior of an adult.

So many of our attitudes, feelings, and ways of looking at things are learned this way, and the process occurs so naturally and automatically that many psychologists believe that modeling is even more important than genetics in explaining why people within the same families are so similar to one another. If someone speaks of getting his hot temper from his father, or explains his shyness by saying he takes after his mother, chances are that the trait was acquired by modeling.

The power of modeling in very young children is especially strong. One child psychologist, Albert Bandura, in an impressive recent study, has shown that children gradually come to exhibit the characteristics even of television characters on programs they watch frequently. They model particular mannerisms and attitudes that they see on the screen; in addition, they most often model themselves after those characters whom they admire, and whom they perceive as being most like themselves.

What is the best way to predict a student's tendency

toward positive or negative attitudes? By looking at the important adults in that student's life, especially his parents. Kids learn to think about themselves not just from what adults tell them about themselves but from watching adults express their own positive or negative feelings of self-worth. Parents with high self-esteem tend to have children with high self-esteem, because their own tendency to feel good about themselves is unconsciously modeled by the child.

Parents or teachers can lecture children endlessly about the need to have self-confidence, but if those adults themselves do not exhibit a postive self-concept, the words are largely wasted. There is an aphorism in child psychology that says "Attitudes are caught, not taught." A positive approach to life is best communicated to the child by exhibiting it, not by lecturing about it.

The upshot of all this for our program in District Two was that we obviously needed adults to feel good about themselves if we were going to have children who did. If children absorb unconsciously whatever the parent or teacher really feels, then we needed to spend time working not only on the children but on the adults as well. The entire psychological climate of Sumter County schools needed to be more positive and more self-accepting. That meant having positive teachers, as well as positive lunchroom workers, maintenance staff, clerical personnel, and administrators.

We were determined to spend whatever time was necessary with our school staffs to put a brighter smile on everyone's face, from the janitor in the smallest rural school to the superintendent. And we wanted all adults who interacted with a student in any way to feel responsible for their attitudes during their contacts with the child. If modeling is as powerful as is claimed, we knew that the attitude of a cafeteria worker who put the liverwurst on a first grader's plate was an important part of the emotional climate in that school—and we wanted that cafeteria worker to believe it too!

The goal in Sumter was to have so many adults modeling positive attitudes that our children would learn those attitudes as naturally as they learned to walk.

When Harvard psychologist B. F. Skinner first began talking about positive reinforcement fifty years ago, he triggered a dramatic shift in the way most educators look at the learning process.

The basic idea of positive reinforcement is as old as man himself. Positive reinforcement is simply another way of describing a reward. People who get good things for doing something tend to do it more often. It's that simple. What Skinner demonstrated was how thoroughly this relationship dominates our lives and, in particular, the development of our personalities in childhood.

Less well known than the role of reward itself is the impressive degree to which positive reinforcement is more effective than negative reinforcement (punishment) in the management of behavior. We all know the familiar example of the donkey that can be motivated to walk forward by either the carrot or the stick. He moves to eat the carrot or to avoid the stick—either method, it seems, is equally effective. But, in reality, the carrot and the stick are *not* equally powerful in getting the behavior we want, whether from a donkey or from a human being.

Rewards are far superior to punishment in the long-term management of behavior. The use of rewards with children not only elicits desired behavior more effectively, it does so with far fewer negative side-effects, and in a far more permanent fashion. Positive reinforcement as a consistent style of parenting, or of classroom instruction, not only gets the job done, it produces a child who feels good about himself, and that good feeling generalizes to every other area of his life.

Unfortunately, the temptation of every parent and teacher is to go for the quick fix, to deal with a disciplinary problem or a difficult situation with the easiest short-term solution, which often includes threats, punishment, ridicule, or harsh criticism. In Sumter, we were determined to curb that very natural adult tendency by becoming aware of the negative and sometimes destructive ways in which we addressed undesirable behavior.

Positive reinforcement takes many forms—a smile, an approving nod or pat on the back, emphasis on correct answers rather than wrong ones, display of projects well done, notes of encouragement on papers, letters sent to parents commending a child's effort and success, and many others. The only limit to the types of positive reinforcement is the imagination of the parent or teacher.

A popular recent book, *The One-Minute Manager,* advocates the practice of "catching people doing something right" and praising them for it. That, in a nutshell, is the principle of positive reinforcement. In the Sumter school system, we referred to that practice as "being a goodfinder." We decided to take the time to discover good things about our kids, point them out, and reward them. We were convinced that every child in Sumter County, no matter how low his grades or bad his record, surely did something well, at least occasionally. Our commitment was to watch that student until we found that good thing, then reward it and cause it to happen more frequently.

*   *   *

With conditioning, modeling, and positive reinforcement as our three tools, we began. If, indeed, we could build stronger senses of self-esteem in our kids by using the right kind of methods, then we vowed we would condition, model, and reinforce like no one in Sumter County, South Carolina, ever had seen before.

10

We spent the first half of 1979 working on a plan to convert the entire school system into positive thinkers. Those spring and summer months were a time of study and planning in the District Two central offices.

When I first announced to my staff what we would be attempting, there was a certain amount of skepticism. That was to be expected. Professional educators have learned to be wary of anyone who shows up at the schoolhouse door with a new approach. So many new ideas have been tried and found wanting that excitement for any novel approach comes slowly. But the early coolness to the idea by some of my staff gradually gave way to genuine enthusiasm.

Changes in my own behavior and that of others in my office subtly took place. We began to use more positive expressions and to be more aware of the presence of negativism in our habits of speech and body language. We raised our expectations for our own performances. The plan was already having an effect on us even as we planned its implementation in the schools.

While the new program was being formulated, I conducted for the board of trustees a series of workshops on the essential ideas of attitude and positive self-image. I had good news and bad news to report to the board that summer: the bad news was that, once again, the students of District Two were below grade-level achievement norms in almost every area that had been assessed that year by the state Department of Education. The good news, I told them, was that we were developing a fresh approach for dealing with the recurrent problem. We would try to upgrade student achievement not with a frontal assault, which had been so unsatisfactory in the past, but by attempting to change the negative emotional climate that we believed to be a primary root cause of the problem.

The board of trustees went for it. Some of them had been as frustrated by the district's pattern of underachievement as I had been, and they were optimistic that my somewhat unconventional plan would work. By the time we adjourned, the board not only had authorized me to proceed with the program but had adopted an official board policy requiring that the development of positive attitudes and self-esteem be a major goal of the school system, to be given priority equal with that of academic development itself! That was a stronger mandate than I had dared hope for.

During the first week of August, we met with the school principals to brief them. Reaction to the plan was very good, and a structure was set up through which each of the principals would contribute to the district office strategies and activities by polling their teachers for suggestions. We wanted to create the largest possible pool of ideas from which to draw as the year progressed. We knew that all good classroom

teachers have many informal ways of building positive attitudes in their students, and we wanted teachers to think about those strategies and pass them on to us, for everyone's potential use.

The key to a good start in the program would be the attitude of the one thousand employees of District Two. It was one thing for the school board and the principals to be with us, but we needed every class-room teacher to share our goals and enthusiasm. But not just the teachers. We wanted everyone who rubbed shoulders with our students to start the school year with a personal determination to make kids feel good about themselves.

To help get these people involved, a staff member suggested we hold a reception for all employees and their spouses immediately prior to the opening of the school year. The idea was to show them they were important and appreciated, and to emphasize, especially to the nonteaching personnel, that they were just as much a part of this undertaking as the academic people. I liked the sound of it, but it would be expensive—several thousand dollars—and we had no budget for such a reception. The board agreed that it was a good idea, but didn't think the taxpayers would approve of such a large expenditure for an unprecedented frill.

We had almost given up on the reception idea when an obvious solution occurred to me: why not ask local businesses to underwrite the cost of this and other parts of the program? We had previously discussed the importance of local merchants and civic leaders being aware of what we were doing. Here was the perfect way to get a businessman's attention: ask him for money!

The next day, I went to see the president of a local

bank. By the time I got to his office, I had decided to ask him not only to pay the tab for the reception but also to underwrite the cost of advertising the program on billboards around town. Why not go for the big bundle? I figured. With all that talk about thinking big, I was beginning to convince myself.

The bank president listened patiently while I made my pitch about the power of self-esteem, the need for a positive school climate, and our planned program. At the end of my little speech, he asked only one question, and it wasn't about educational theory.

"How much?" he asked me.

I swallowed one quick time and gave him the figure. He didn't even hesitate. "We'll do it," he promised. "It's the kind of program we need around here." And just like that the money was ours.

We could now set in motion a reception for motivating the motivators. Three weeks later, on the night before school began, we entertained almost two thousand people. We had a big banner made with the slogan EVERYBODY WANTS TO BE SOMEBODY—EVERYBODY IS SOMEBODY! to decorate the reception site. We had great food, name tags, terrific music, and, best of all, no speakers!

The next day, we met with the district's teachers to present the plan to them. The enthusiasm and good feeling from the night before had carried over, and the session was positive and upbeat. A group of music teachers from around the school district dug up an old pop tune of the forties that speaks of "accentuating the positive" and "eliminating the negative." The revival of this old song, familiar to many, was such a hit that it became the unofficial theme song of District Two, and we sang it over and over during the next two years. Some of the younger teachers and virtually all the students had never heard the song, and gave us undeserved credit for writing the lyrics on the spot to fit our program!

There is always a risk with a new educational program that the teachers in a school system will dismiss it as a gimmick and ignore the whole thing. I knew there were many veteran teachers in our system who might understandably resist our approach as too simplistic to be taken seriously. The influence of well-regarded teachers in any given school is such that our program would have no chance of succeeding if they sniffed at it as beneath their professional dignity. To their credit, the teachers embraced the program from the very beginning—most of them not only went along with it, but set out conscientiously to make it work. As an added incentive, at the meeting the teachers were notified that a part of our staff development plan would permit them to receive graduate credit, as well as credit toward their mandatory recertification, for participating in the program.

The teachers' meeting was an unqualified success. Some people stayed at the school to talk about the program for as long as two hours after we adjourned. We had distributed bumper stickers with positive slogans to the teachers in the meeting, and many of them put them on their cars before leaving the parking lot. One teacher with over twenty years' experience came to me after the session, asked me to autograph her printed program, and said she felt better about herself that night than she had in twenty years in the classroom.

The next afternoon, the nonprofessional staff was reminded that their influence was especially critical. We told the clerical personnel how important it was for them to contribute to the overall positive climate of the schools. A secretary, I stressed, is more than just a secretary when her office is in a school; she is a model for every student who enters her work area. We wanted the offices in our schools to be the most inviting places in town, and our secretaries to be positive and self-confident role models. Their response was enthusiastic.

Lunchroom workers were similarly challenged, as were employees on the custodial and janitorial staffs. In fact, I explained to the custodial employees that they were spending more on supplies than we believed to be necessary to keep a building in top-notch condition. To encourage them to reduce waste, I announced that we would take whatever they saved on supplies and put it into their salaries as an incentive plan. It worked so successfully that our school district was written up in a procedural handbook for custodians and janitors in school systems across the state.

We finally had done all we could do to motivate the motivators. The District Two personnel had heard the plan and were ready to try it. It was time now for students to pour through the doors of our schools to begin a new year, and for us to find out if we knew what we were doing.

11

I have a tendency to get carried away talking about the theory and principles of our PMA program. Sometimes people stop me in mid-sentence and say, "Okay, Dr. Mitchell, that's very interesting, but exactly what did you *do*?"

Conditioning, modeling, and positive reinforcement—that's what we did. School kids in Sumter, South Carolina, could hardly move during 1979 and 1980 without bumping into a reminder of their potential to do great things. We missed no opportunities to tell them and show them.

• Billboards with short positive-thinking messages went up around town shortly before school began.

• Every day in each school began with contemporary music played over the intercom system—songs with upbeat lyrics that conveyed the message of self-worth and the ability of people to win against great odds.

• In each classroom in the elementary grades, and in the homerooms at the secondary schools, the teacher began the school day by reading "attitude boosters" to the students. These were short, positive messages that were written and submitted by students, teachers, administrators, and parents. We edited and compiled them in the district office and distributed them each month to the school—one booster for each school day that month. The teachers would take a few minutes to discuss these ideas with the students before beginning the day. A typical booster: "Believe in yourself! Don't ask for help until you have tried every way you know to solve a problem. You will be surprised at how many problems you can solve on your own!"

• Bumper stickers with positive slogans were distributed to students, parents, and people in the community.

• Every school set aside special bulletin boards for positive thoughts and ideas. In many schools, contests were conducted to select the best bulletin board design, or competitions were held between classes for the same purpose. The point was not only to have the bulletin boards always promoting the right kind of ideas, but also to involve the students themselves in thinking about and formulating these slogans.

• Laminated book covers, always popular items with school kids, were printed with positive-attitude messages and distributed to students free. The cost was borne by local businesses.

• A PMA logo was developed for the school system and used on school letterheads, postage meters, all school supplies, whatever we could find to put it on.

• Attitude boosters were taped and aired on local radio stations. We started with a single station, WDXY radio, and asked if they would donate airtime; within a few weeks, four other stations in the area had offered to air the tapes also. We took a month's supply of the boosters by WDXY, their DJs recorded them, and the stations broadcasted them four times a day. The boosters were up to thirty seconds in length.

• The popularity of radio boosters led to video boosters on the Florence, South Carolina, television station which served Sumter. TV boosters were aired twice daily, as a public service, in addition to a thirty-minute monthly program. These video boosters eventually included spots taped especially for us by such people as Bob Hope and Olympic gold medalist Bruce Jenner— at no cost, of course.

• All our telephones in the school system were answered with "We're having a *great* day in District Two . . . or Cherryvale School . . ." or wherever. People all over the country commented on our telephone greeting, and we believe even that small reminder made a difference. (Not everyone's day was brightened by this bit of cheeriness, incidentally. One gentleman caller responded to the greeting grumpily: "Damn it, there's no way *every* day is a great day." Our receptionist replied sweetly, "Sir, you just try missing one and see." He hung up.)

• Some of the schools began having pep rallies the day prior to achievement tests and other major exams. The idea was to emphasize, as athletic events are emphasized, the importance of academic performance and to counter somewhat the fear of test taking. The entire student body would gather in the auditorium or gym while cheerleaders cheered, pep bands played, and banners and posters proclaimed things like, "BE A GOOD TEST TAKER! YOU CAN DO IT!" Students loved these "academic pep rallies," and teachers enjoyed them, too.

• We even put the food to work! Lunchroom workers baked fortune cookies with short PMA slogans, printed on small slips of paper, baked inside. In addition, over nine thousand cartons of milk, printed with

"confidence builders," were distributed each day as simple reminders that a student was someone special.
 • Teachers were asked to make lists of all the negative expressions they used or heard others use. We then made a list of positive substitutes for those common negative expressions and circulated the lists to school personnel and parents. We wanted everyone to become more conscious of the negative tone of our communications with students, and to try whenever possible to rephrase our messages in more constructive ways.

Occasionally, I would hear someone in the community complain that we were trying to "brainwash" our kids in District Two. The constant drumbeat of positive attitudes seemed to make a few people nervous, as if somehow we were going to talk some poor child into doing well against his will. But criticism of that sort was infrequent and gave us no pause at all. I always responded the same way: "Yes, in a way we are brainwashing our kids. We're trying to wash their brains clean of negative thoughts and attitudes so they can enjoy this great world!"

The most exciting part of our program was designed to bring outstanding models of success to our community in order to tell us of the importance of positive attitudes in their own lives. We wanted these meetings to attract students, parents, teachers, and even local people who were otherwise uninvolved in the school system.

Each meeting was designed to be a happening, an event that would get the attention of everyone in Sumter County. Lively music and entertainment always accompanied speakers who were glamorous as well as good models of PMA principles. We called these giant rallies our mountaintop experiences, because we intended them to be memorable occasions for our impressionable young students. The first year, we had five of these rallies and included among the speakers someone with whom all our students—black or white, girl or boy, scholar or athlete—could identify.

The first of these meetings was in September and featured one of the nation's best motivational speakers, Zig Ziglar. Officials from South Carolina's state government, along with city and county officials, joined a crowd of twenty-five hundred. People aged six to ninety-six listened to Ziglar's highly charged you-can-do-it message, and I knew from the human vibrations there that afternoon that we were on the right track.

The pattern for the other rallies was the same as in that first meeting. Principals and faculties from each of the schools sat together, and parents were invited to join them if they wished. We selected a mix of elementary and secondary students to participate in the program along with teachers and principals. A maintenance worker gave the invocation. The behavior of the hundreds—and later thousands—of students was excellent on every occasion.

School bands and choruses were an important part of these programs. In addition to our "Accentuate the Positive" theme, which was always played at the conclusion of the program, other upbeat, positive themes were played and sung. Performing at the events was considered an honor, not a chore, by the various students who were selected to sing and play. One third grader communicated the tone of the experience when she wrote to her teacher, "I liked the program, but when we stood up to sing, my legs were shaking. But I said, 'I can do it.' Thank you for letting me sing."

That little girl was obviously getting the message.

After the first rally, the momentum of the program built steadily, and crowds for the events grew to over five thousand before the year was over. To Sumter we brought a first-rate lineup of speakers. Olympic gold medalist Bob Richards, once a world record holder in the pole vault, talked about the role of self-belief in athletics. Marilyn VanDerber, a former Miss America, was an especially popular guest. William Raspberry, a nationally syndicated columnist for *The Washington Post,* came to Sumter to speak, then returned to his newspaper to write about the kids he met there.

Undoubtedly the guest who made the biggest impact was Dr. Norman Vincent Peale. This grand old man of positive thinking, still energetic and forceful in his eighties, held the attention of even the youngsters in the enormous crowd. All had been exposed to PMA ideas enough by that time that they realized they were seeing and hearing a legendary figure, and they soaked up every word he said. He told them of his own childhood, of being afflicted by shyness, self-doubt, and feelings of inferiority, until one day he decided to do something about it. His testimony was an unforgettable moment.

There was a powerful positive energy being generated in Sumter District Two, and something Dr. Peale said to me that evening testified to it in a way I'll never forget. As I took him to the airport, Dr. Peale told me how impressed he had been with our students, and how moved by their attitudes and warmth. "Dr. Mitchell," he said, "when I came here today my cup had run dry. But what I saw in those children has filled it up to overflowing. Thanks for letting me be a part of what is happening here in Sumter County."

There was something happening in Sumter County, and though it would be several months before we would see the results in statistical test data, we could already feel it in the air.

12

I f the giant rallies were the dessert in our PMA diet, then the meat and potatoes were the work being done on a daily basis by teachers in the classrooms and parents at home.

We realized that no combination of billboards, milk cartons, and show-biz techniques alone would do the job of upgrading the attitudes of ten thousand students. The best we could achieve with bumper stickers and speeches would be to call attention to the role of attitudes and perhaps create a better climate in which a good teacher or parent could produce the results we desired. If there were heroes in the miracle of District Two, they were not Norman Vincent Peale or the local bank president—they were the hundreds of classroom teachers who spent all day, every day, trying to find ways to build self-esteem in their students.

Early in the program, I saw indications that teachers were rising to the challenge, and students were feeling the difference. In November, in an in-service training program with teachers, the moderator of the session interviewed six schoolchildren about self-concept and attitudes, and we were all startled to see just how much these second and third graders had already learned about the power of positive attitudes. It was as if each child had had his own personal Mrs. McIndoe pouring confidence into him.

After the youngsters were interviewed, the teachers heard from a few high school students who had been asked to tell about their experiences. None of us anticipated the emotional appeal we heard from a handsome young teen-ager who told of the frustrations of his parents' divorce, of leaving his friends in another state to relocate in Sumter, and his slow slide into drug abuse. As five hundred-plus teachers listened intently, he told of a bungled suicide attempt and the acute depression that had begun to lift as he listened to the message, "Everybody is somebody—we care!"

The things he was hearing in school and the warmth he felt from his teachers had gotten through to him, he said, and he had discontinued his drug use and was trying to make the most of his potential. He ended by expressing, in a moving statement, his gratitude to the teachers who along the way had let him know they cared. I believe every teacher left the auditorium that day with a desire to be a teacher who cares, really cares, for students.

The teachers themselves were expressing their care in many different ways. We had "goodfinder" cards printed for elementary teachers, who would use them to jot down positive things their students did during the school day as reminders to praise those students specifically for those behaviors. They then wrote personal notes to parents—thousands of notes went out that year—telling the parent about the good things done by the child.

A teacher, we found, could write a personal, handwritten note of three or four sentences in fewer than three minutes, including addressing and sealing the envelope. For a teacher with thirty students, one such note each day—three minutes a day—would mean one note per month to the parents of each child, telling them of a specific good behavior by their child. The resulting impact on the parents' attitude toward the child was enormous.

Teachers in the secondary grades gave their students printed sheets with lines and check-off boxes for "Positive things to do today," and designed special rewards for completing the sheets.

Teachers frequently told me of small classroom victories that they attributed to our new emphasis. One elementary teacher told me of her second-grade student who was unable to read. She discovered he had a great interest in music, so she discontinued his reading group to give him extra time in music; her plan was to try to build his positive attitudes before tackling his reading problem. She reasoned that he had convinced himself that he could not read, and his negative attitude was thwarting everything she tried to do with him. In addition, he showed an unhealthy distrust of teachers as well as a negative attitude toward himself.

So she played to his strength. She assisted him in making a drum, bought some records he liked, and read music books to him. For three straight weeks, she held him out of his reading group while giving him large doses of self-confidence. His trust for her improved rapidly; he began to exhibit greater willingness to cooperate with her. She then began talking to him about the need to read in order to enjoy different kinds of music. She gave him private reading lessons in small doses and a big helping of music, until gradually he became one of the best readers in the class and rejoined the regular schedule.

As I went from school to school in the district, looking in on classrooms and talking with students, I could clearly see that the teachers were doing their part. It was inspiring to see students as young as five years old involved in PMA activities planned each week by the faculties. I heard kids sing PMA songs, listened to poems they had written, and saw their artwork on display. I would walk into a classroom and hear primary students who could recite the "attitude boosters" verbatim. Most of all, it was thrilling to see the positive interaction between the teachers and the students— teachers who were expressing love, caring, warmth, and genuine interest in the children.

I tried to show my appreciation for the heroic job these teachers were doing by taking the time to write personal notes myself—not to parents, in my case, but to teachers whose exceptional work came to my attention. So much good news poured into the district office that I was kept busy maintaining that commitment; my secretary told me I averaged over fifty letters per week, and I never used a form letter. I wanted the letters to be personal notes of appreciation and gratitude for specific behaviors.

One day in a planning session, one of the teachers told the group that she had received a letter from me thanking her for special contribution to the PMA program. She had been so pleased to get a letter from the superintendent that she had shared the news with some of her colleagues, and several of them had replied that they had also received letters from me. *Aha!* they thought. They decided to meet in the faculty lounge after school to compare notes and see if they had gotten the same letter. When they met and found that they had not received form letters after all, but that each was a personal letter, they were surprised— and a little embarrassed—at the negative conclusion to which they had all jumped!

They need not have suspected me. I have never cared for form letters, and I was more convinced than ever, after hearing that story, that I would never use one.

But with the kind of teachers we had in District Two that year, why should I? They were the frontline troops in the battle to turn our school system around, and we owed the gains we were making to them. One teacher gave me a quotation—she called it her favorite—that might well describe the attitude so many of her colleagues adopted that year. It is from the late Haim Ginott, an outstanding child psychologist and teacher:

> I've come to the frightening conclusion that I am the decisive element in the classroom. It is my personal approach that creates the climate. It is my daily mood that makes the weather. As a teacher I possess a tremendous power to make a child's life miserable or joyous. I can be a tool of torture or an instrument of inspiration.

13

etting parents involved in the program was a bigger challenge, since, unlike students and staff, they were not with us on an all-day everyday basis.

The community rallies and media blitz helped to some degree, but to implement our program, we developed a series of positive parenting seminars in various schools in the district. Anyone who has worked with local PTA groups knows how difficult it is to get a crowd of decent size to attend workshops or training sessions in the school. Unless there is a musical or dramatic program in which Junior is participating, or awards are being given and little Ginger is receiving one, Dad and Mom are likely to ignore the meeting.

With that in mind—and with too little practicing of the positivism that we so zealously preached—we made plans for three hundred fifty to four hundred people at our first positive parenting seminar. When the evening arrived, we had to scurry to accommodate an overflow crowd of over six hundred parents. Part of the crowd was diverted to the school library to watch on closed-circuit television, and many people stood against the walls and even in the hallways throughout the session.

Each parent went home that night with a packet of material containing information on How to Be a Positive Parent. Our primary message to the parents at the outset of the program was summed up by this letter, which went to every parent in the district:

Dear Parent:

Recent studies have shown a definite relationship between self-concept, which is the way an individual sees himself, and classroom performance.

Since our goal is to have students perform as well in the classroom as they can, we believe that helping them feel good about themselves and the work they are doing will help accomplish that goal. We can do this by treating students as worthy individuals and by reinforcing the positive aspects of their school responsibilities.

We are asking that you, as parents, join hands with us in this endeavor so that your children will receive maximum benefit.

Since consistency is a necessary ingredient of any successful venture, we feel the home and school should work together in similar and complementary activities. We are certain that many good things of this nature are already taking place in our homes. However, for parents who wish assistance in improving the self-concept of their children, we are happy to furnish the attached suggestions and materials for your use. You will notice that some apply only to children of certain ages, while others apply to all ages.

We urge you to contact teachers for more specific ways of helping in this endeavor. Please join us in our efforts to help your children develop a positive and realistic self-concept that will carry them successfully through life.

The number of parents attending our positive parenting seminars continued to increase after that first session. The programs were varied, with students and teachers often working together in the workshops. In each of them, we urged parents to commit to seven basic practices, which we felt are fundamental to every home, regardless of the age or ability level of the child.

These seven principles are the building blocks on which positive parenting depends:

1. Say something encouraging and complimentary to your child each day.
2. In your home, create a warm, friendly atmosphere where smiles abound.
3. Always have a listening ear and a feeling heart. Make every effort to have your child feel he is important to you and is a worthy member of your family.
4. If your child fails in some endeavor, help him understand that there are many ways that he has been successful, and that failure may turn to success by trying again.
5. Treat each child as an individual; do not expect the same performance for all.
6. Help your child understand that although you may dislike some specific behavior, you do not disapprove of him as a person.
7. Ascertain your child's needs for attention and recognition and meet them. Each individual needs a certain amount of attention and recognition, and when this need is met in a positive

and friendly manner, the necessity for gaining attention in a negative way is greatly diminished or eliminated.

Though these rather obvious principles are familiar and habitually practiced in some homes, we realized that many parents had never heard them expressed in any orderly way, and we hoped to start such parents thinking about them. Many middle- and upper-middle-class parents in Sumter had always approached parenting in a rather systematic fashion, but it is the nature of the public school system to deal with the entire range of parental styles.

It is impossible, of course, to raise the awareness of those parents who need it most by singling them out in some way as bad or negligent parents. The only way to reach them is for all the parents in the community to participate together in discussing and expressing a few basic principles of parenting—even if, for some of them, those ideas are elementary and unoriginal. If the parents who are already relating positively to their children ignore the program because it represents nothing new to them, our program would be seen as remedial help for unfit parents, and of course no one would participate. The entire attempt to teach positive parenting would collapse. Fortunately, that did not happen in Sumter Country. Ignoring our program never became the fashionable thing to do among the better-educated parents in our community, and as a result, the overall level of parental consciousness was raised.

We also made wide use of another set of principles, which, we felt, were valuable reminders for every home in the district, from the superintendent's right on down. We posed these in the form of a set of questions, which we recommended be placed in a prominent spot in every home:

AS A FAMILY, DO WE . . .
share our feelings with one another?
talk with, not at, one another?
practice courtesy and civility with one another?
encourage everyone to stand up for his own ideas?
act in ways that say we trust and love one another?
give one another the chance to make mistakes without penalty?
help one another to succeed?
take joy in one another's successes?

We knew that homes in which the answers to these questions are yes, even most of the time, are almost certain to produce children who, by the time they enter the schoolroom door, are already well on the way to being positive people.

14

The results of District Two's two-year PMA program extended beyond an improvement in student performance, which had been the original target, to include other areas of our school and community environment.

Not just the kids, but the adults in District Two as well, were affected by the program. Somewhat to my surprise, I first began to see it among the maintenance staff. At one of the early PMA rallies, I noticed our maintenance men were dressed in coats and ties. That may seem a small thing, but I was a bit taken aback to see these men without their familiar coveralls and work clothes. They were on duty, after all, and not there for an evening out.

I remarked to the director of maintenance that his men looked sharp, and he responded, "Dr. Mitchell, this PMA program has instilled pride in our men and our department. We have more respect for ourselves and feel better about who we are and what we do than ever before." He told me the men had brought their coats and ties to wear to the rally, and would change back into work clothes before taking down the stage and removing the chairs.

A few days later, I visited the maintenance department at the district office and noticed a big sign on the wall. It read, BETTER MAINTENANCE THROUGH A POSITIVE ATTITUDE. Before the year ended, our maintenance and custodial employees were featured in a statewide publication because of the schools' exceptional state of general cleanliness and neatness. What an unexpected spinoff benefit! We started out to get higher achievement from our kids, and along the way got better work out of our janitors as well.

Once, while I was visiting an elementary school, a custodian approached me and asked if we could talk for a moment. We went into an empty classroom and sat down. He told me that all his life he had felt ashamed of who he was and what he did. He had always held simple, unskilled jobs and believed that since he had been born poor and was uneducated in a formal sense he was destined to spend his life doing unskilled labor. This year, he said, he had learned that he could choose his attitudes, and that those attitudes could determine how he felt about himself and his job.

He had begun to take pride in his work, he told me, and had decided to do what would have been, a year earlier, an unthinkable thing—he had enrolled in an adult education course. He was enjoying it, just for the fun of learning new things, and was happier than ever before. "For the first time, Dr. Mitchell," he said, "I'm enjoying going to work every day."

Many teachers had similar experiences during those two years. One veteran teacher told me that during one academic pep rally held prior to exams, she had faced up to her own fear of taking tests and realized that fear was the reason she had never pursued a master's degree. She had decided then and there to go after it and was now enrolled in a graduate degree program.

During this time, a sizable number of our teachers were notified that their certification would expire and that they would be required to take a test, the National Teacher's Examination, to have their teaching credentials renewed. This group included some of our most outstanding teachers, but many of them had an extreme fear of the exam, knowing that their teaching certificates and ultimately their jobs depended on passing it.

I have always been personally on record as opposing the use of this exam as the single criterion by which a veteran teacher could be dismissed from the classroom, but it was the state law. After the teachers and I commiserated, we decided to approach the problem by dealing directly with their fear of the test and the possible consequences of failing it: we designed a workshop in overcoming the fear of failure. Taught by a member of the central staff, the workshop emphasized the uses of positive mental attitude that we were teaching our students. Having participated in that series of workshops, the teachers took the national exam, and we had the lowest number of failures we had ever had since the test was mandated by the state Department of Education.

The impact of an improved emotional climate was demonstrated graphically in another instance involving our teachers. Two teachers in the district had been chronically unable to maintain discipline in their classrooms and, as a consequence, were advised that their contracts would not be renewed for the following year. Both asked for an opportunity to respond to the terminations. Although the chance was granted, like any

gun-shy administrator who has made a tough personnel decision, I feared angry outbursts and bad feelings
all around.

It didn't turn out that way. The first teacher, a
young woman just out of college, told me she recog-
nized her shortcomings in controlling children in her
class and emphasized that she was not in the office to
protest the action. She said she had come in to express
her appreciation for having a chance to gain experience, and to tell me how much she had personally
benefited from the PMA program.

The second teacher, a middle-aged man, had a similar mission. His problem in imposing discipline in his
classes, he said, was a weakness that he was determined to correct. He accepted the dismissal as a necessary action and said he only wished to state that the
PMA program had prepared him to accept this apparent failure with poise and graciousness.

When the board of trustees declared that an official
goal of our schools would be building positive attitudes, it affirmed a belief I have had since my career as
an educator began. I have never felt that it made much
sense to teach kids how to do multiplication tables if
we never teach them how to cope with everyday life.

Many years ago, a poignant statement by an anony-
mous high school English teacher received consider-
able publicity. It makes its point in a memorable way:

> I have taught young people for ten years. Dur-
> ing that time I have given assignments, among
> others, to a murderer, an evangelist, a boxer, and
> a thief.
>
> The murderer was a quiet little boy who sat in
> the front seat and regarded me with pale blue
> eyes; the evangelist, easily the most popular boy in

school, had the lead in the junior play; the boxer lounged by the window and let loose at intervals a raucous laugh that startled the geraniums; the thief was a lighthearted Lothario with a song on his lips.

The murderer awaits death in the state penitentiary; the evangelist has lain a year now in the cemetery; the boxer lost an eye in a brawl in Hong Kong; and the thief, by standing on tiptoe, can see the windows of my classroom from the county jail.

All these pupils once sat in my room, sat and looked at me across worn brown desks. I must have been a great help to these pupils—for I taught them the rhyming scheme of the Elizabethan sonnet and how to diagram a complex sentence.

What a graphic reminder that we do not teach subjects, but students! It is a distinction that is easily overlooked, especially in this day when the public is calling for more attention to basic skills in the public school curriculum. There is a saying that we are not just the teachers of academic subjects but also the teachers of life. One encounter near the end of that 1979–80 school year made me feel that in the teaching of life, as well as academic subjects, we were making an impact.

I was relaxing at home one evening when the phone rang and I took a call from a young man whom I had not met. He said he needed to talk with someone and asked if he could come to my house. When he arrived, he told me that he had tried for three weeks to muster the courage to call and ask to see me.

He was a dropout from one of our schools and had become involved in dealing drugs. He had been on his way to a nearby college campus one night three weeks earlier, he said, and quite by chance had heard me on a local radio station talking about the power of attitudes, and the ability we have to change our lives by changing our attitudes. "It was like a light switching on," he told me. "I had been unhappy with the way I was living, but I thought there was really no way to change." As he listened to that radio show, he realized that the dangerous course his life had taken was a result of his negative and hostile attitudes toward himself and many other people, but that he could choose to change those attitudes and begin moving in another direction.

So that was why he had come. Having poured out his story, he stopped rather abruptly. "There it is, Dr. Mitchell. I'm here to ask you to show me how to change my attitudes, so I can change my life." For the next several hours, I tried to answer his questions, and before he left the house that night, he vowed to try to make a new start. He wanted something to read during the next few days, so I let him borrow the two best books I know for a young man trying to turn his life around. As a public school official, I gave him a copy of *The Power of Positive Thinking;* as a private citizen who happens to be a Christian, I gave him the New Testament.

He became a student of both books. The last I heard of him, he had gotten a job and had made a complete change in his outlook and his life-style. His story is an example of the payoffs of our PMA program that has nothing to do with "the rhyming scheme of the Elizabethan sonnet and how to diagram a complex sentence."

15

When the results of our yearlong effort were in, they showed that the tangible academic gains of the PMA program were just as impressive as the intangible personal ones.

The most important single indicator was our students' performance on the standardized achievement tests used in the state, the Comprehensive Test of Basic Skills. Comparisons of our overall performance in 1979–80 with that of previous years, as well as comparisons with state and national averages, showed conclusively that indeed, we had registered substantial gains during the PMA time period. In grade-level equivalents, many of the district schools tested more than a full year of academic growth ahead of the previous year. This increase occurred in the individual subject areas as well as in total battery scores.

One of the most dramatic outcomes was that, for the entire district, the grade-equivalent mean score for District Two first graders was above the national average. This was the first time that had occurred since such records had been kept.

Generally, increases were greatest for the elementary grades, a result that supported our feeling that the PMA program was the primary cause of the gains. Reading scores for first graders, for example, were up in virtually every school, in some cases dramatically so. In St. John School, a rural, all-black school, first-grade reading scores improved from .7 in 1978–79 to 1.7 for the 1979–80 year, an enormous jump.

What this meant, interpreted informally, was that kids finishing the first grade in 1978–79 were reading at a level that might be expected of them after seven months of school, putting them behind the target schedule and substantially behind the national average. At the end of our PMA year, however, first graders in that same school were reading as if they had been in school a year and seven months, which was well ahead of the target schedule and ahead of the national average as well.

At another predominantly black elementary school (R. E. Davis), grade-equivalent means were above the national average for both first and second graders. At Davis, the most dramatic gain was for third graders: the percentage of third graders performing above the national average in reading jumped from 9.8 percent to 49.2 percent in just one year.

Could such an increase be the work of a single extraordinary teacher at Davis, perhaps? Someone who may have arrived the same year as the PMA program? That was not the case, and, in fact, other schools also showed enormous gains in third-grade reading. At Mayesville Elementary, the percentage of third graders reading above the national average increased from 13.7 percent to 41.4 percent. Second graders at Mayesville, not to be outdone, increased more than a full grade level for their total battery of scores.

Though reading scores probably were the single area with the most impressive gains, overall performance in basic subject tests also improved throughout the system. District Two third graders, for example, scored higher in basic subject tests from 1979 to 1980, with a significantly large percentage of them performing in the upper two quartiles on national norms. In one elementary school, Shaw Heights, the 1980 test results showed increases over the 1979 tests in every single subject area.

Another way of looking at our students' performance is to note that in all schools combined, grades three through six inclusive, District Two kids increased the percentage of students in the upper two quartiles more appreciably than did the state as a whole.

High school and junior high school students showed improvement in academic performance also. Some of our high schools showed increases in every area over the grade-equivalent means from the 1979 tests. Reading scores for ninth graders and eleventh graders went up a full year on a grade-equivalent basis during the PMA program.

At Furman High School, the percentage of tenth graders performing above the national average rose from 29.2 percent to 42.8 percent in overall testing. They gained two full years in reading scores, and a year and a half in language skills.

At Hillcrest High School, where the rate of pupil turnover was greatest because of the large number of Air Force families, tenth graders scored approximately one year higher in every subject area on the Comprehensive Test of Basic Skills.

Apart from national test scores, our own grading within the district reflected better classroom performance. At the end of the year, the total number of failures by grades and by subject areas was lower than in any previous year for which we had records.

There were measurable payoffs for our PMA efforts in areas other than classroom achievement. For example, discipline problems decreased across the system. In previous years, poor discipline had been one of the trademarks of our district. At the end of the 1979–80 year, our school principals reported that teachers were assuming more responsibility for handling their own discipline cases in the classroom and were referring fewer cases to the principal's office. While the greater improvement in discipline appeared to be taking place in the elementary grades, reduction of disciplinary actions occurred in the high schools as well. By the end of the year, the overall rate of suspensions in the system had dropped from 458 a month to 70 per month.

One of our schools, Ebenezer Junior High, had a particular reputation in the Sumter County area for its lack of discipline. As the PMA year progressed, the principal and teachers there reported to me that many of the students who had caused disciplinary problems were participating in school life in a more positive way. The change at Ebenezer was so dramatic that at the end of the year, the school was selected by the state department of education as one of the three most improved schools in discipline in the state.

We were especially hopeful that the self-esteem emphasis in District Two would make an impact on our students who were involved in drug and alcohol abuse. The district's counselors tested these students for self-concept during the year, and, while there was no significant measurable change in self-concept for these individuals, there was a system-wide reduction in the referrals for drugs- and other substance-abuse problems.

Vandalism has always been a major problem—and a major expense—in District Two, as it is in public schools around the country. (Recent national statistics show that each year some 250,000 cases of vandalism occur in public schools, at a cost of over $200 *million!*) In previous years, window-glass breakage alone had cost Sumter County $30,000 annually. During the first two years of the PMA program, no cases of school vandalism were reported in District Two. Not one! That single result may be the most impressive outcome of the entire campaign, and certainly it saved the county more money than the total cost of the program.

Absenteeism also declined during the PMA program. During the four years prior to 1979–80, we had experienced attendance increases at the rate of approximately one percent each year. The year of our self-esteem emphasis, though, we *more than doubled* that rate of increase; for the first time in the district's history, our absenteeism was below the South Carolina state average, with an attendance increase of 2.3 percent.

Student participation in school activities also improved during the year. Most of our music teachers, for example, felt that the opportunities for performing publicly, which were so greatly increased by the PMA program, had stimulated involvement in band and chorus. We saw a big increase in enrollment in these programs the next year. At Ebenezer Junior High, for example, the size of the chorus increased from 45 members to 135 members. System-wide, the district's secondary schools had sixteen members selected as all-state chorus winners, the largest number ever to be so honored.

Things improved even in the athletic area. In one high school especially, Hillcrest High, simply winning a game had been itself a rare event. In the years since the PMA program, the school not only has had winning seasons but has won regional and state championships. It would be difficult to prove the PMA effort contributed to that, but the athletes and coaches are convinced that that was what turned their athletic fortunes around. They learned how to believe in themselves, they say, and that is what made the difference.

In reporting these remarkable changes in District Two, I must temper my enthusiasm somewhat by emphasizing that this one program, implemented for one or two years, will not make a permanent difference in District Two or any other school system. Will the improvements last? people ask me. The answer is that they will not last unless the program continues.

"Motivation is like taking a bath," Norman Vincent Peale has said: "One won't last a lifetime!"

Unfortunately, there is no "quick fix" for the problems of low self-esteem in our school kids. It is not reasonable to take one or two years to tell a child he is worthwhile and expect the message to survive fourteen or sixteen years of negative conditioning. If the gains we made in Sumter County are to endure, the effort to build our kids' sense of personal value must also endure.

Another point that must be emphasized is that the impact of our program clearly was greatest on the youngest children. For students in the early elementary grades, whose sense of themselves is less rigidly formed, the gains we measured were enormous. As one goes up the range of ages and grades, the difficulty of producing change increases accordingly. A fifteen-year-old student has already developed attitudinal habits, often negative ones, and it is much more difficult to reverse these than to build the positive habit in the first place.

Can you imagine the potential we would have if first and second graders, who soaked up our self-esteem training like little sponges, could get a steady diet of positive conditioning, modeling, and reinforcement for five years at home, then for twelve more years in the public schools? Only when this happens will we see what is the true potential of a systematic program of teaching self-esteem.

During the two years after we started this program in Sumter, we tested all our students for feelings of self-esteem and compared their scores with scores on the Comprehensive Test of Basic Skills for the same students. We found exactly what the self-esteem literature predicts: students who scored highest on self-esteem also were our highest achievers, and this held true at all grade levels. The relationshp between self-esteem and academic achievement was high in every grade.

The Sumter District Two experiment in applying positive attitudes in the school must be considered, by almost any yardstick, an unqualified success. But any short-term program is, of course, only a short-term solution. At best, it shows what can be done, and what must be done in an ongoing manner, to make our schools and homes fertile ground for the growth of productive, positive adults.

Dr. Helen Billings, founder of the Montessori Institute of America, observed our program and its results and rendered this judgment: "It has worked miracles for an increasing number of people, and it has just begun to grow. It could be the catalyst for changing the entire country."

16

The results of the Sumter experience, impressive as they are, barely hint at the enormous potential that will be tapped when more extensive programs are put into practice in school systems nationwide. And even then, the good that can be achieved by educators is relatively small compared to that which parents, using similar approaches, can achieve in their own homes.

In one respect even the best efforts of educators are too little and too late in the development of a child's self-concept. By the time we first meet the child at age five or six, the time of his greatest susceptibility to attitude training has passed. Obviously, the impact schools make still is worth the effort. The memory of my own personal development is evidence enough of that, and reason enough for me to keep trying to make McIndoes and Mintos out of the teachers with whom I work. But the most powerful teachers of self-concept, for good or for ill, are not teachers, but parents. Parents *are* the teachers of life.

Dr. Peale has written of a meeting held by the National Education Association at which the presidents of many of the country's most important universities were present. The purpose of the meeting was to discuss what education could do about the country's most pressing need. And what was that most pressing need? More scientific education to compete with the Russians? More space education? Better training in economics? Not at all: those educators agreed that the most pressing need of this nation is a happy and substantial homelife. Create health in the home, they said, and that health will radiate outward, touching business, industry, education, government, and every other phase of society.

As we turned our attention to the attitudes and values of Sumter students, even those of us who had been in public education for many years were amazed to see how often the home environment was the best predictor of a child's sense of self-worth. This relationship had little to do with race, economic status, or any other demographic category. Some parents, even though they had no formal education or professional success themselves, seemed to know what to do to produce children with high levels of self-esteem. And others, with every apparent socioeconomic advantage, did not.

Carl Rogers, whom some consider to be the greatest living psychologist in America, once made this observation:

> I am beginning to feel that the key to the human being is the attitude with which his parents have regarded him. If the child is lucky enough to have parents who have felt proud of him, wanted him, wanted him just as he was, this child grows into adulthood with self-confidence

and self-esteem. He goes forth in life feeling sure of himself, strong, able to lick what confronts him. If a child grows up in this unconditionally accepted atmosphere, he emerges strong and sure, and he can approach life and its vicissitudes with courage and confidence.

When the schools have that kind of individual to work with, the task of public educators becomes an easy one. We can then focus our energies on maintaining the student's positive self-view and not be forced to attempt a radical reconstruction of an already negative self-image. Unfortunately, the school is too often a repair shop, not a place for fine tuning. The sad reality is that if a parent depends on the school to do the job of building self-esteem, the job probably will not be done.

The perfect arrangement, of course, is a partnership between parents and schools, with the school serving merely as an extension and reinforcer of what is happening at home. In an essay entitled "Quality in Education," the Educational Policies Commission states, "Among the most important influences on the effectiveness of teaching is the overall concern, guidance, discipline, and affection of the parents. The standards parents set and the attitudes they express have a decisive influence on a child's progress."

While he was in Sumter to speak to employees and students in 1981, *Washington Post* columnist William Raspberry told us of an experiment in Washington that supports the idea that it is parents, not educators, who are potentially the most effective teachers of self-esteem. Frances Hughes, principal of an inner-city middle school, started with the premise we had in Sumter: if poor self-concept equals poor performance, improved self-concept ought to result in improved academic performance. The question was how to improve self-concept.

In contrast to our strategy at Sumter, Ms. Hughes decided to try working directly through the parents. That approach made sense, she felt, because it promised to produce results that were more general (one parent may have more than one child in more than one school) and more permanent than working through teachers, since any teacher is with a particular child for no more than one year.

She pretested a group of seventh-grade youngsters, who were performing below grade level, for the adequacy of their self-concept. She then took their parents and divided them into three groups: one, a controlled group that was identified and given no further attention; a second that met regularly, with access to school resources but without a structured program; and a third that got her full treatment. She had no further contact with the children for the next thirteen weeks, during which time she and her staff of counselors, aides, and specialists worked directly with the parents.

The full treatment referred to consisted of teaching parents to transmit to their children, at home, what the parents themselves had learned in special evening classes designed to help them cope successfully with their own personal problems. At the end of that period, she again tested the children for their self-concept. The post-test results revealed statistically significant differences between the unstructured group and the controlled group and also between the structured and unstructured groups. Ms. Hughes attributed the results to the parents becoming highly motivated and to the immediate boost to their self-esteem. They, then, began immediately to transmit this newfound self-esteem to their children.

This Washington, D.C., experiment suggests not only that parents can be effective in raising the self-esteem levels of their kids but also that it is never too late to begin—even at the relatively advanced stage of the seventh grader. It might also suggest that the best expenditure of time would be to teach parents, not teachers, about self-esteem. As deeply as I am involved in the public school system, I would be hard-pressed to argue against that: if we could have either one, and only one, engaged in self-esteem training, the parent is undoubtedly the more potent teacher.

Fortunately, we need not make that choice. Positive parenting, combined with a school system that makes self-esteem training one of its chief priorities, is a partnership that almost guarantees self-confident and able youngsters. In reflecting on the Sumter experiment, in fact, I have often speculated that perhaps the program's success was chiefly due not to anything we did directly in the schools but to the heightened attention of the district's parents to self-concept principles.

An unknown poet once described the partnership this way:

I dreamed I stood in a studio
And watched two sculptors there.
The clay they used was a young child's mind
And they fashioned it with care.

One was a teacher—the tools she used
Were book, music, and art.
The other, a parent, worked with a guiding hand
And a gentle, loving heart.

Day after day, the teacher toiled with touch
That was careful, deft, and sure.
While the parent labored by his side
And polished and smoothed it o'er.

17

I am the father of two sons, and when I begin talking about the partnership of schools and parents in developing a child's attitudes, I tend to think more as a parent than as a school superintendent. Speaking strictly as an educator, however, I have a few concerns that I think are fundamental to that partnership. If I were at the blackboard, and every parent in America was seated at a desk before me, here is the first appeal I would chalk up on the board: *don't give up on the public schools!*

There has been an erosion of confidence in public schools among this generation; new private schools and academies are sprouting like spring mushrooms all over the country. Parents are afraid of crime in the public schools, the breakdown of discipline, and the influence of drug abusers on their children. In addition, many conservative, religious parents have become concerned about what they call an antireligious bias in the curriculum of public schools and are sending their kids to private schools, hoping to protect them from antireligious teaching.

As much as I can understand these parental fears, I must argue emphatically that, in almost every case, the fears far exceed the reality. The problem of crime in the classroom is usually not as severe in any local situation as it is reported in the media. Public officials, no doubt meaning well, sometimes add to this over-blown furor over the breakdown of school discipline. With such major attention being given to public school problems, it is understandable that a conscientious parent might consider it worth the extra expense to pull the child out of a public school and put him in a private academy.

Middle-class America simply cannot afford to abandon its public schools. In a pluralistic, melting-pot society such as ours, having the common meeting ground of public schools—where young people can learn to relate to people different from themselves, to tolerate different viewpoints, to cope with unfamiliar perspectives—is a fundamental need. The public schools will always be a microcosm of the world as it really is, and the best true education a youngster can receive is to learn to function well in it.

In most cases, parents who remove their children from public schools do no one a favor, least of all their children. My challenge to parents who feel their public system is a bad one—either academically or otherwise—is to stay in the system and change it, improve it. Literally millions of parents have spent untold amounts of time and money over the past twenty years starting private schools because of their fears about public education. Imagine how much better off our children would be today if those same parents had organized themselves and spent that same effort making a difference in the public schools where they lived!

Unfortunately, the worst public relations problems we have in public education are of our own making.

We seem to have a sort of institutional death wish in public schools, always talking about our problems, our challenges, the things that are going wrong. Having felt for so long that the public schools, like death and taxes, are forever, we have acquired habits of unbridled criticism of our schools, and it is our own criticisms that are largely responsible for creating the current crisis of confidence in our schools. As the cartoon character Pogo says, "We have met the enemy and he is us!"

I was speaking recently to a group of parents in Allegany County, Maryland, where I presently serve as school superintendent. After the meeting, a young mother waited to speak with me. "Dr. Mitchell," she said, "my child has been enrolled in your school system only since September. My husband had been furloughed from his job, and when I knew we had to take our child out of private school, I cried for two weeks. I just want you to know that what we thought was going to be a disaster turned out to be one of the best things in our life. I have never seen my child so self-confident, so happy, and so productive. She is really a totally different child since enrolling in your school system."

I am convinced that the worst times of public school deterioration have bottomed out, and we are already regaining the confidence of parents in public education. If the parents who truly care about their children will stay with us, we will get the job done.

The second point I would make to parents on my blackboard is the following: *remember that teachers— and principals—are human, too.*

I have dealt with teachers from all the various angles: I have been a teacher myself; I have been a parent who was happy or unhappy with my child's teacher; and I have been the principal and superintendent responsible for hiring, inspiring, and occasionally, firing the teacher.

In all these years, in all these various roles, the one understanding that has emerged most forcefully is that the teacher is human, too. There are good and bad teachers, kind and not so kind, experienced and inexperienced teachers, but they are all people, and what one gets from them in the classroom is inseparable from what they are feeling as individual flesh-and-blood persons. Far too often, parents overlook that obvious fact, which is unfair to the teacher and the child he teaches.

In a *Wall Street Journal* article on public education, one high school English teacher from Pennsylvania was quoted as saying; "Teachers are very fragile, dedicated people. They receive very little praise throughout their careers—from students, from parents, or from administrators. Thus, to keep on teaching, they must develop their own self-confidence, fed mostly from within. Then, poof! slash! rip! sap! Nearly ninety percent of them are told they don't measure up. That aura of confidence is shattered."

The mechanism of positive thinking must work in a giant circle, or it does not work at all. If the teacher who faces your child every day has not been helped to feel good about himself, it is much less likely that he can build your child's feeling of self-worth. Teachers who are positively reinforced are better teachers, and the parent can reinforce that teacher more effectively than the principal or even a student can. Mark Twain once remarked that he could live for two months on a good compliment, and most teachers would agree!

In the Sumter positive thinking program and in Allegany County, Maryland, we in the district offices constantly reminded ourselves to be sensitive to the needs of each teacher as a human being, because it is with that teacher's own personal state of mind that the entire process of positive attitudes begins. Even superintendents, however, are prone to forget this simple truth, and of that I, too, am guilty. Occasionally I am reminded with a jolt. One afternoon, a teacher came unexpectedly into my office. She sat down, looking as wild and distraught as I have ever seen a teacher look. With no small talk or preamble, she pleaded. "If you really want to help me become a positive person, you have to loan me thirty-six dollars to pay my light bill before five o'clock or they will cut off my electricity!"

I was startled by the unusual appeal, so suddenly and emotionally delivered. Yet, the look on the teacher's face was so filled with pain that I hardly thought about what I was doing; I reached into my desk drawer, pulled out my personal checkbook, and wrote her a check for thirty-six dollars. "I hope this will help you," I said rather lamely, as it sank in that what I was doing violated specific rules and policy set by the board of education. She jumped up, grabbed the check, and was gone—no "Thank you," "Good-bye," or anything.

Three months after this peculiar incident, the teacher came back to my office. I had not heard from her at all in those three months. She was returning, she said, to explain her behavior and apologize for her rudeness that day, and to pay back the thirty-six dollars. "I want to tell you a story," she said softly, and it was quite a story.

"My husband had deserted me and my children just before this happened," she began. "He took all our money. I was humiliated and completely broke. I had borrowed all I could from the credit union and had no money and nowhere to get any. I had to pay my light bill that day or the power company was going to cut off our electricity. That was the last straw. I was absolutely at the breaking point." She continued her story, telling me that she had loaded her husband's gun and was determined to kill herself. As she sat on her bed, she said, a thought "went through my mind—'Dr. Mitchell says everybody is somebody.' That thought froze me. I decided I would come to your office and see if you would help me."

She had put the gun in her purse and come to the district office ready to kill herself if she were, as she put it, "rejected one last time." She got the money, survived the immediate crisis, and went on. Things started getting better after that, she said—still not 100 percent, but definitely getting better—and she knew she was going to make it.

I got more than my thirty-six dollars back that day; I got a dramatic reminder that teachers are human, too—not robots or teaching machines, but people with their own personal crises and needs. After that woman left my office, a realization came to me again and again: that day, in all her pressure and pain, that woman had sat in front of a classroom full of kids and tried to teach them that life is a wonderful, positive experience. We expect a lot from our teachers, and the least we owe them is to recognize their humanness.

Superman and Superwoman do not work in your child's classroom. The teacher who is there, from whom we parents expect so much, needs to know that parents understand that.

My third appeal to parents is a simple one: *get involved without getting in the way.*

There is probably no more conventional bit of advice than this, but it is so important I must briefly repeat it.

The school needs the involvement of parents like automobiles need gasoline. They just won't run very far without it.

In many cases, the school will call on parents for specific kinds of help, and my strong feeling is that parents who do not respond have little ground for complaint when things don't go well. PTAs and other parent groups, chaperones and car-pool drivers for field trips, band booster clubs, volunteer workers at special events—in these and many other ways, parents' involvement is solicited. In most schools, I have noticed that the same group of parents usually responds to every call. What is needed in most schools is a broader range of parental participation, not only to get the jobs done but to demonstrate to students that their school life is a community concern that is widely supported by more than a few parents with time on their hands.

Apart from these structured situations in which the school calls on the parents, I believe it is important for the parent to take the initiative to get involved in matters more personally related to his own child. Very rarely does a parent inquire about a child's classroom performance more often than the teacher would desire. Many parents, sincerely eager not to pester the teacher, operate with far too little specific information about how the child is doing or what is expected by the teacher.

"Is there anything I can do to help?" is never considered a hostile question by a good teacher. And, if you as a parent mean it and are genuinely willing to take on any job that needs doing, you'll be surprised at how often the answer will be "Yes, thanks, there is something we need!"

Even if the school cannot utilize your efforts in any

particular part of its program, your child will not miss the implications of your willingness to try. You are communicating to the child, in another small way, that his school is important to you, which means that he is important to you, which means that he must be somebody!

18

There is no such thing as instant parenting.

Most jobs can be delegated, but positive parenting is not one of them. This is a task that the busy executive can't assign to a staff member. No secretary can cover for him on this one. Being a positive father must be done personally, in the flesh, and it takes lots of time—there are no shortcuts.

Being a positive mother takes attention, lots of it, even when the modern woman has a job of her own and a to-do list that seems never to get done. This is one thing her family needs that can't be bought in the frozen food department and popped into the microwave.

When we make a commitment to be positive parents, we are signing away large chunks of our time, and no one has yet figured out how to do it any other way.

For children who are developing a sense of how important they are, we communicate an important message with every decision we make about the use of our time with them. Five minutes taken out of a busy father's day to call home and chat with a preschool daughter is more than just a conversation—it is a powerful message to a little girl that she is an important person. When two parents cancel a social evening to attend a son's Little League ball game, they are telling him something about his basic self-worth.

For busy adults, time is the currency of exchange. Most parents have more disposable money than disposable time; time is a more valuable commodity, and our children know it at some instinctual level. We give time to those things we feel are really important, and if that does not include our kids, they get the signal, loud and clear.

When we are deciding whether or not to invest our time in something, the pragmatic questions we ask are, "What will I be doing there? What will my presence achieve? What will I actually *do* during this period of time if I allocate it to this particular thing?" These questions are usually a sensible test of whether something is worth spending time on it. But when our kids are involved, these may be the wrong questions entirely. The more relevant question is this: "What will I be saying to my child by spending time in this fashion?"

Most often, when we spend time on his pursuits, we are saying to the child, "You are a person of value. You have great worth. What you do matters to me."

The importance of time spent with our kids is not just in what we do while with them but in what it teaches them about their self-worth. I saw a news item about Jack Nicklaus, the pro golfer, in the paper a few years ago. The article reported he had passed up a major golf tournament, which might have been worth many thousands of dollars to him, in order to watch his son's Florida State University football team play a rather ordinary game. I can only guess at what personal considerations may have produced that decision, but I was struck by the statement Nicklaus was making—simply by being there—about his estimation of his son's worth. Busy parents must find occasions to make that statement, if they are serious about positive parenting.

My own life got so hectic at one stage that I almost forgot that point. I was in my last year of graduate school, writing a dissertation, studying for comprehensive exams, and teaching classes at the University of Alabama. My son Mike was a youngster in elementary school at the time. Gradually, as the school year passed, he became more and more reluctant to go to school each day.

Being positive-thinker types, my wife and I would brush aside his complaints about school and send him off each morning assuring him it would be a good day. But each afternoon, he came home an emotional wreck, discouraged and unhappy. I had so much pressure at the university, and so little time, that I let this condition continue for a long period, until finally I was forced to take off a few hours and go to his school to see what the problem was.

The principal had set up a conference for Carolyn and me to meet Mike's teacher, and it didn't take long to see why Mike was in such bad shape. His teacher was probably the most negative individual I have ever met; to even the untrained eye she was a full-blown neurotic, clearly unfit to teach small children. After that conference, in a meeting with the principal, we learned that he was aware of the problem and had already begun termination procedures. "Obviously," he told us with chagrin, "she doesn't like herself or her students very much."

Eventually, Mike and his classmates got a new teacher, and he recovered his good spirits about school, but the immediate result of the meeting with his previous teacher was that I was able, for the first time, to understand his feelings and know how to help him. Had I not taken the time to put aside my own agenda for half a day and address his problem, I never would have known why he felt as he did. I often have looked back on that time and thought how close I came to committing the unpardonable sin of being too busy to find out about what was going on in a difficult period in my son's life.

One of the common beliefs of modern parents is that if the basic needs of the child are being met, if the logistical details of food, transportation, and baby-sitting are covered, the responsibilities of parenting are met. (I heard recently about a gadget invented by a man in Connecticut: a time clock that doles out a predetermined allowance to a child, daily or weekly, while his parents are away from home!) Again, the crucial question is not "Am I really needed there?" but rather "What does my being there—or being absent—say to the child about how important he is?"

Another common misconception is that the important time to spend with one's kids is at the big events in their lives—birthdays, graduations, holidays, special ceremonies when the child is performing or receiving recognition of some sort. These events are indeed important to the child, but in a curious way children don't seem to give the parent much credit for being there at these times—about the best the parent can do is to avoid the child's unspoken censure for being absent. If the event is a special one, the child tends to think of the parent's presence as obligatory and discount the value of it.

On the other hand, the parent who makes an effort to be with a child at unexpected times, to show up at the child's activities when he really isn't expected, to arrange a special time together for no particular reason, affirms the child's importance. "You don't have to have a birthday, or receive an award, or be the starting pitcher for me to take time for you," the parent is saying. "Being with you is important to me because you are important to me."

Lee Salk, a well-known psychiatrist, in a book about fathers and sons, described his experience with his own father: "Caring is one thing. I mean, my father cared more about us than anything in the world, but he cared from afar. What matters is to be there on a daily basis."

Dr. Charles Paul Conn, a developmental psychologist, who assisted me in writing this book, has observed: "With children, there is sometimes no substitute for parental time—periods of unhurried, undivided attention. Often, even the best parents forget that need, or develop life-styles which provide no room for it. We find ourselves so problem-oriented as parents that we spend most of our time with our children as troubleshooters. When our child needs our help, whether to tie his shoe or to get a driver's license, we address the problem, help as best we can, and move on. But often there is no particular thing our children need from us; what they need is just for us to be there."

Sometimes parents are so busy that time carved from their schedules is an extremely valuable commodity, and their children usually know it. In an ironic way, that gives the especially busy parent an edge—it lends greater impact to the time spent with the child. If Dad's time is truly precious, spending it on Junior makes an even stronger statement than ever.

Many years ago, I read a charming story about a young man named Johnny Lingo, who lived in a primitive culture in which a young man desiring a particular maiden for his bride bargained with her father. The fathers of the village demanded payment for their daughters, and the usual form of such payment was cows. In those days, two or three cows would buy an above-average wife, and four or five a very beatiuful one indeed.

Johnny Lingo was the brightest, strongest, handsomest young man in the village. He was fond of a young maiden named Sarita and set out to ask her father to bless their union. Sarita could most generously be described as plain; she was not truly ugly, but she was not very attractive either. Shy and frightened of her own voice, she was afraid to speak up or to laugh in public. But Johnny Lingo loved her and went to bargain for her with her father.

The villagers' favorite sport, at such a time, was to gossip and speculate over how many cows would be paid for a bride, and in this case, the betting was that it would be two cows, three at most. It was whispered that Sarita's father might even settle for one cow, since Johnny Lingo was the shrewdest trader in the village and Sarita was a bit older than most maidens at their marriage date. But when the time came, Johnny went into the tent, walked straight up to the father, grasped his hand, and said, "Father of Sarita, I offer eight cows for your daughter."

The village was astonished. It was the highest price ever paid for a bride, even one of great beauty; but Johnny Lingo was as good as his word, immediately producing the eight cows in payment, and the wedding was held that same evening.

As the story goes, Sarita underwent a startling transformation. Within months, her bearing was like a queen, the sparkle in her eyes was dazzling, she moved with striking grace and poise. People who came to the village, who had not known her before, called

Sarita the most beautiful woman they had ever seen.

Much later, someone thought to ask Johnny Lingo why he had paid such a price. Smart trader that he was, why would he offer eight cows for a woman he could have had for three? Did he do it just to make Sarita happy?

"Happy?" he responded. "I wanted Sarita to be happy, yes, but I wanted more than that. Many things can change a woman. Things that happen inside, things that happen outside. But the thing that matters most is what she thinks about herself. Before, Sarita believed she was worth nothing. Now she knows she is worth more than any other woman in the village. I wanted to marry Sarita. I loved her and no other woman." He paused and smiled again. "But I wanted an eight-cow wife."

19

I n our positive parenting programs, we picked up some specific ideas that may be helpful in developing your child's self-esteem. Some of these suggestions are suitable for young children and some for older ones; others are adaptable to any age. I make no claim to originality. They are simply extensions of the ideas that have been tried and found successful. In no particular order, I suggest a few of them.

Use Television Positively

Television, a favorite whipping boy of parents and educators for the past quarter century, can be an asset in positive parenting. The most obvious use of TV is as a carrot in a parent's scheme of positive reinforcement. It makes an ideal reward to be withheld or delivered contingent upon the child's other behaviors. This strategy breaks down if the child comes to feel that TV watching is a right rather than a privilege. If a parent establishes a rule—no TV until homework is done, for example—it is critically important that the rule be observed consistently. Making frequent exceptions has two undesirable outcomes: it teaches the child that rules can be broken and it shifts the focus of responsibility from the child's behavior, where it should be, to the parent's generosity. The child blames the parent's intractability, rather than his own poor performance, for his inability to watch TV on those occasions when the rule is enforced.

Another way in which television can be useful to the positive parent is as a springboard for parent-child discussion. To the young child, TV is a window on the world, and the parent should intersperse periods of television watching with periods of conversation in which the child is encouraged to describe and interpret that world to the parent. Simply being asked to summarize, in two or three minutes, the story that he has just seen on television is a valuable exercise for the young child. Even commercials can be used in this way, especially with older children. As you watch with your kids, you can help them become constructive critics of commercials. You can even take turns predicting what will happen next in situation comedies or action-adventure shows.

The main thing is to talk. Television is at its worst when it anesthetizes the child so he sits numbly watching hour after hour. If you watch with the child, and let the TV be the backdrop against which you and your child enjoy a stream of verbal exchange, even the most banal and silly show can be used positively. Moreover, making constructive use of television does not require force-feeding your child a steady diet of educational TV, as some parents think. Even *The Dukes of Hazzard,* combined with a little positive parenting, can have some redeeming value!

Be an Unpredictable Note Writer

Write brief, breezy notes to your child, expressing your pleasure at having such a terrific kid! Put them in the child's schoolbooks, lunch bucket, with his gym clothes, or anyplace they are sure to be found. These notes may specifically address something going on in the child's life that day ("You look super in that skirt, honey! See you at 3:30!"), or reflect on something that happened earlier ("I was just looking at some old pictures of our trip to New York. Didn't we have fun! I love you!"), or looking forward to something in the future ("Hey, this is Thursday. Only one more day to the weekend! How about a movie on Saturday?").

A parent in Cumberland, Maryland, tried this idea and told me how it worked for her: "My daughter was doing badly in mathematics and didn't like it at all. After we began stressing positive students in our school, I got an idea. I started putting little notes in her math book every morning. They would say things like this: 'You are smart, and I know you can learn math,' or 'I believe in you, and you can do it.' After a while, she started making better grades and started getting more confidence in herself. Then she started leaving me notes around the house. They would go something like this: 'I know I can learn math now because you believe in me.' Her grades have improved drastically and her whole outlook on the subject has changed. She enjoys her math class now and feels so much better about herself."

One of the keys to this strategy is the unpredictability of the notes. If the child comes to expect a note every day, same place, same message, the whole exercise becomes ho-hum for you and the child, and loses its effectiveness. Don't do it every day, but do it frequently. (And don't expect too much from it; the extraordinary case of the Cumberland mother is an unusual result. It doesn't happen that way very often.)

If No One Tells You Something Good About Your Child, Ask!

In our programs in our school system, we encourage our teachers to be "goodfinders," to spot something worth complimenting in each child's behavior and write notes to parents telling about it. If this kind of thing is already happening in your child's school, you are in a rare situation and don't need to read this paragraph at all. If, however, you never receive such a note or call from your primary-level child's teacher or principal, you can still make the "goodfinder" system work. The only difference is that you yourself have to find out something good about your child to pass on to him. All it requires is a telephone and a willingness to risk being thought a pushy parent. Try it! Call that second-grade teacher and simply say, "I'd like to help Suzy feel better about herself by sharing something good I've heard about her from you. Could you please help me with this?" Chances are the teacher will be able to think of something; the worst that could happen is being asked to wait a day or two while the teacher watches for something to share.

Of course, this strategy works best with younger children—a high school senior is not likely to appreciate his mother calling around Central High fishing for compliments for her boy. And certainly it is more effective the more specific the behaviors you can comment on. "George is a sweet little boy" won't have much impact, especially not after the first time or two.

Make Positive Thinking a Game

Most children and teen-agers love games of all kinds, and there are many ways to make positive thinking into word games that can be played in the car while traveling or at other times when you are all together with nothing else to dominate the conversation. For example, a friend of mine reports that his children (ages seven, ten, and twelve) enjoy a game in which he concocts horribly negative hypothetical situations, and they take turns trying to give positive responses to the situations. A warning: this requires a certain light-heartedness in your approach to PMA itself. Especially with teen-agers, there will be a tendency in such games to parody the Pollyanna-like attitudes of unrealistic positive thinking, and the parent who takes it all too seriously may not wish to open himself up to that.

Even while spoofing and laughing at PMA stereo-types, though, the child is learning that attitudes are a matter of choice, that one can respond to bad news either constructively or negatively. That is the lesson the parent wishes to teach, and sometimes a game is a good way to teach it.

Another such game for older teen-agers involves establishing a fund into which everyone pays a fine for the offense of using any particular negative words that have been mutually declared to be off limits. The fund should be earmarked in advance for some frivolous purpose once a certain sum is reached. Everyone in the family participates and monitors one another's language. When anyone errs, the fine is paid on the spot.

A high school band director in Tyrone, Pennsylvania, where a PMA program is under way, told me that he has such a system in his band. The dirty word in this case is *can't*; any student who uses that word pays a dime into the PMA pot, which will be used for a band party at the end of each semester.

Show Your Child How to Say Thanks

Urge your child to select one person who has meant something positive in his life and write that person a short, unsolicited letter expressing appreciation. This becomes doubly valuable if the whole family will sit down at the same time and do it together, Dad and Mom and each of the children writing individual letters to different people. Let the children have the widest possible latitude in selecting the recipient, and let them decide whether or not they wish to share the contents of their letters with you. In this activity, you are both teaching and modeling appreciation, as well as structuring an occasion for all of you to reflect on the positive things that other people have brought into your lives.

In our school system in Maryland last year, we did this on a system-wide basis, with all our students, teachers, and even our nonteaching employees sitting down and writing a letter to someone who has been important to them in a positive way. The students were required to write their letters as a classroom exercise, but they were given the option of mailing the letters or merely discarding them. In one school, out of approximately six hundred students, more than five hundred letters were mailed to what were undoubtedly many surprised people all around the country. At the conclusion of this activity, many of the adults who participated told me it was the first time in many years they had taken the time to write to someone for no reason except to say, "Thanks for what you have meant to me. Your life has been a blessing to mine."

Having your children do this, and doing it with them, will achieve three things: (1) it will teach them to express gratitude; (2) it will remind them that we owe our well-being to many other people; and (3) it will, in many cases, provoke a response from the recipient of the letter which in turn will further reinforce the child for his positive behavior.

20

The single most effective way a parent enhances his child's self-esteem development is by maintaining a home environment that accentuates the positive. And though we all accept the impossibility of totally "eliminating the negative," as the old song puts it, there are ways of ensuring that negative realities do not dominate the emotional landscape of one's home.

How does a parent do this? By using in the home the three tools we use in our PMA program to achieve the same purpose: conditioning, modeling, and positive reinforcement.

The *conditioning of positive attitudes* in the home involves constantly offering to the child statements about his self-worth, reminders of his tremendous potential, and an unswerving emphasis on whatever is good in his life at any given time.

This takes a conscious effort by even the most naturally positive parent. Most of us would be surprised if we could see how much of our speech is negative. In the 1982–83 school year, I challenged teachers and members of our office staff to monitor their own conversation flow for a few days to see what percentage of their casual comments and ordinary language was essentially negative in its tone. Each of us saw that we had underestimated considerably the degree of negativism in our own daily activities.

Maintaining a steady emphasis on the positive side of life gets to be a habit, but acquiring such a habit takes a little effort. Obviously, life has its bad moments, and only a fool refuses to recognize them. Being positive does not mean ignoring unpleasant realities. A parent who is so determined to be positive that he masks his honest feelings of disappointment, anxiety, or sadness does not communicate to his child the positive joy of life—he communicates instead that the parent is a bit on the dotty side. Or, worse yet, that he is a phony, always faking a smile just to make a point about positive thinking.

That is obviously not constructive, for the parent or the child. The positive parent makes no attempt to obscure the fact that negative things do exist; but neither does he dwell on that negative reality. The positive parent looks past how bad things are to remind the child of whatever brighter, more hopeful other realities also exist. It is a matter of emphasis. Being positive with one's kids means looking at things realistically, but consistently putting a positive spin on the matter at hand.

One of my favorite stories is of two shoe salesmen who were sent to a newly discovered island that was inhabited by primitive natives. The salesman from one shoe company quickly wired to his home office: SEND PLANE BACK TO PICK ME UP. NO BUSINESS POSSIBLE HERE. NATIVES DO NOT WEAR SHOES. But the salesman from the other shoe company wired his company this message: SEND SHOES, LOTS OF THEM, ALL SIZES, STYLES,

COLORS. NONE OF NATIVES CURRENTLY WEARING SHOES. UNLIMITED OPPORTUNITY.

The breakfast table in every home is a perfect place for general grumpiness. Almost no one gets up on a school day feeling great. Everyone is sleepy; there are aches and pains; the kitchen floor is cold; breakfast cereal is the same as ever; homework is not finished; the weather is lousy—every day, at every breakfast table in the country, there are numerous negative things upon which to comment. This is where the positive parent sets the tone for his children for that day. When Dad and Mom have cheerful expressions, talk about good things that might happen during the day, and gently deflect the glum, early-morning complaints, the mood of the occasion can swing upward for the whole family. Children are not likely to provide the initiative, nor should they be expected to do so. But they can gradually come to practice positive courtesy—even at the breakfast table on a dreary school day—if they live with parents who set that example.

This consistent modeling of positive attitudes is the most critical part of the conditioning process in the home. When the parent does not merely tell the child to be positive but demonstrates it, the message eventually gets through. A mother who puts little happy faces on the refrigerator door, plants positive notes in her daughter's school lunch, sticks posters with PMA slogans around the house—but fails to act out those attitudes in an ongoing way with her kids—can hardly expect a have a positive child.

Children can be exceptionally sensitive to the true feelings that underlie an adult's professed attitude. A parent who dutifully engages in a forced cheeriness, when in reality he is preoccupied with his own fears and anxieties, rarely convinces the child. Positive thinking as a life-style gains credibility with children, especially as they grow older, when parents are open with them about financial difficulties, job insecurity, illness, or other challenges the family faces. A child cannot measure the full meaning of a parent's positive example unless he understands the context of negative possibilities in which that attitude occurs.

For the same reasons, it is important to let children know about the parents' own struggles and failures as teen-agers and young adults. In talking with kids about their parents, I have been amazed at the number of children who have little knowledge of the humble beginnings and heroic accomplishments of their own parents. Some of the best real-life examples of winning against great odds can be found right in our own homes, and it is a shameful waste for children not to be aware of them.

A father who experienced reverses and disappointments in his early career should not be reluctant, either through a sense of modesty or a reluctance to appear boastful, to discuss those times with his children. Once we have made it through the challenges, survived the tough times, and now are comfortably successful, it is tempting to consign the story of our early struggles to the past. We forget that our children see us as having always been the competent, self-confident achievers we finally became, and sometimes we want them to see us that way.

However, the child is cheated when we take that posture. He needs to know that once you were a scared kid yourself, that once you were self-conscious about your background, or your inability to keep up with the other kids in your class, or the size of your nose. When a little boy asks his father, "Were you ever scared, Daddy?" he wants the answer to be yes, because he is scared himself sometimes. When a daughter asks,

"Did you ever not get asked to the prom, Mother?" she hopes the answer is yes—if a woman as poised and lovely as her mother once hoped just to be asked to dance, then maybe things will turn out well for her!

A parent's task is comprised of thousands of small, on-course corrections of the child's behavior. If the child is to learn by doing, it is inevitable that what he does will often be done incorrectly, and the parent's job is to point out his error and show him a better way. On a day-in, day-out basis, this can get to be a grind. A mother sometimes feels her only function in the life of little Tommy is to play domestic policewoman—"Stop doing this," "Quit acting that way," "No, Tommy, that's not how to behave."

The daily fabric of parent-child interaction must unavoidably include a large amount of correction, making it all the more crucial that the parent develop habits of responding to a child's small daily failures and successes in a positive style. For example, two children are outside playing, and their play takes them near, around, and ultimately into a mud puddle. One child's mother shouts to her dirty youngster, "You'd better get in this house right now! Look at you! You're filthy!" The other mother, with an equally muddy child, says, "Come on, Jane, let's go get cleaned up. I'll help you look all pretty again."

Sometimes we tend to control children's behavior through fear, obviously because fear is such an effective short-term motivator. For example, a mother sees her child pick up a dirty jar from the garden and drink from it: "Don't drink that dirty water. You'll get a disease and die!" Instead she might use a more positive approach: "Let's go inside and get a clean glass for you."

When I became a young adult and first began to

think analytically about my poor self-concept, I real-ized for the first time how much of my behavior in childhood had been motivated by fear. At home I was afraid of punishment. My grandmother used to tell us tales of dark forces in the woods that came to get un-ruly children. "You'd better act right or the bogeyman will get you!" Or sometimes it was the hogeymaw who was lurking somewhere in the dark to punish bad little boys. At school I was afraid of being embarrassed, and of failing. At church I was afraid of hellfire and brim-stone. Most of my life was dominated by fear of one sort or another.

The use of fear, threat, and reprimand to correct a child's behavior is easy and immediately effective, but the long-term result can be a fearful child who lacks self-confidence. There is research that shows that any form of negative reinforcement from adults decreases the child's self-image more sharply than positive rein-forcement increases it. In other words, criticism pro-duces a negative impact greater than the positive impact of praise. The parent who feels he is doling out equal amounts of criticism and praise is not having that effect at all, since the two do not balance out in the experience of the child.

To have a child who understands realistically both the positive and negative sides of life, who has a bal-anced sense of his strengths and his weaknesses, it is necessary to overload on the positive side! When we scold a child once and praise him once, the balance sheet, unfortunately, is not even. The child must have a predominantly positive diet of adult feedback to emerge as a healthy, well-balanced adult himself.

I don't know when I first saw this simple poem and cannot now find who wrote it, but it illustrates very well the choice we have to respond positively or nega-tively to our children:

"I got two A's," the small boy said.
His voice was filled with glee.
His father very bluntly asked,
"Why didn't you get three?"

"Mom I've got the dishes done,"
The girl called from the door.
Her mother very calmly said,
"Did you sweep the floor?"

"I mowed the grass," the tall boy said,
"And put the mower away."
His father asked him with a shrug,
"Did you clean off the clay?"

The children in the house next door
Seemed happy and content.
The same things happened over there,
But this is how it went:

"I got two A's," the small boy said.
His voice was filled with glee.
His father proudly said, "That's great;
I'm glad you belong to me."

"Mom, I've got the dishes done,"
The girl called from the door.
Her mother smiled and softly said,
"Each day I love you more."

"I've mowed the grass," the tall boy said,
"And put the mower away."
His father answered with much joy,
"You've made my happy day."

Children deserve a little praise
For tasks they're asked to do,
If they're to lead a happy life,
So much depends on you.

It won't win any prizes for poetry, but it makes the point very well. Many parents, who have such high standards and positive expectations for their kids, will find themselves in the first twelve lines. In our desire for a child to have and become the very best, it is possible to communicate only that we are impossible to please, that the child's behavior is never quite good enough to earn our unqualified approval.

The challenge is to be a "goodfinder," however erratic or frustrating the child's behavior. The positive parent is constantly looking for something good, finding it, and rewarding it with no strings attached.

21

Positive attitudes alone will not ensure your child a successful school experience. It does little good for him to have positive feelings about himself and the world around him if he fails to acquire certain basic intellectual skills. Though it is not original with me, I like to refer to this combination as the "new ABC's of learning: Attitude, Basic Skills, and Competence." They go hand-in-hand, complementing and reinforcing one another.

Reading is the most basic of the academic skills, and in almost all our studies, it was shown to be more sensitive to a child's self-esteem than any other. Some educational psychologists contend that the best single predictor of a third grader's reading success is his level of self-esteem upon entering school.

The intervention of parents in a child's education is perhaps more important—and potentially more fruitful—in the area of reading than in any other. Because the child's self-concept is in the formative stage and susceptible to alteration in the preschool period, and because reading is so basic to all other learning, parents can make a more substantial impact here than in any other area of the child's schooling. Unfortunately, over twenty-three million Americans can't read the label on a can of soup. They are functionally illiterate—and most of them are products of the public school system.

There are some simple things a parent can do to give the preschooler a head start in learning to read and acquiring the other cognitive skills that are based on it. My wife, Carolyn, frequently recited nursery rhymes to our boys, even while they were all out shopping or buying groceries. Talking to your child, simply but intelligently, while you feed and bathe him, even before he is apparently old enough to understand all you are saying, is part of establishing a rich verbal environment in your home.

Reading to your child as early and as often as possible is also fundamental to his development. There are numerous payoffs for this investment of your time:

• Your child will see that you value reading and will like reading because he feels you do.

• Reading to your child requires period of undistracted time with him, which is itself important.

• The child's verbal skills will improve as you encourage him to describe pictures he sees.

• Pictures will help develop his visual skills and learn to translate pictures into words.

• Reading to the child will teach him that reading is recreational, that it is fun, and not a job to be done.

Hold your preschool child in your lap while you read to him from picture books, making sure the pictures are interesting enough to hold the child's attention while you read the contents of that page. Point to the pictures and describe them. When you are reading stories, rather than nursery rhymes or poems, stop to paraphrase the stories and talk about them. Encourage the child to respond, and positively reinforce whatever comments he makes.

With very young children, it may be necessary to present a simplified paraphrase, but it is also important to read what is actually on the page. Keeping the stories short, bright, and upbeat will make the child an eager listener. But be careful not to overdose—it is easy for overzealous parents to be so determined to do this kind of thing right, and to do enough of it, that it becomes a chore for both parent and child. Keep it light, and keep it fun for both of you.

Fathers sometimes regard reading to children as something of a maternal activity and fail to do their share of it. That is a mistake, and one that I made when our sons were small; I had the old-fashioned idea that my time with the boys should be spent primarily in physical activities, while Carolyn read to them. The child, and in particular the son, may get the same verbal training from the mother, but he also gains the unfortunate notion that reading is something done mainly by women, which may eventually reduce his likelihood of becoming an active and enthusiastic reader.

Here are some tips for developing reading skills in your preschooler:

- *One to two years of age.* Start early. Remember that the first five years are the most important in developing self-concept in your child. Talk in positive, upbeat language to him. Use books with large and familiar pictures, such as animals, automobiles, children, common household objects, etc. Use repetition in reciting and reading nursery rhymes and children's poems. Let your child turn the pages of the book as you point out things about the pictures and describe them to the child. If he gets tired, quit. Build up the child's interest layer by layer, minute by minute.

• *Two to three years of age.* Find books with short stories and pictures the child can relate to; also use make-believe stories, encouraging the child to use his imagination. Read books the child especially enjoys over and over, commenting on new things about the story each time. Ask the child to repeat things about the story to you.

• *Three to four years of age.* Find and read books that use a lot of repetition and rhyming, as well as the sounds of various animals and objects. Have your child say these sounds with you. Before you reach the end of the story, ask him how he thinks it will end, encouraging him to use his imagination and also be part of the book. He should be able to listen about ten minutes at a time at this age, but, as when he was younger, quit at the first sign he is tiring.

• *Four to five years of age.* Buy picture books that are a little longer and go into more detail than when the child was younger. Read books that have sequels, and show the child the relationship and sequence of the books. Let him make up words that rhyme, using nonsense words when he wishes. Read books about community helpers, books about firemen, policemen, doctors, and so on. Read stories about how things happen—for example, how a butterfly is formed in a cocoon. When you are driving in a car with the child, point out different shapes of road signs, tell him what the signs say, and make a game of having him identify them to you later. While grocery shopping, read labels of cans and boxes to your child.

• *Five to six years of age.* In reading storybooks, let the child decide what could happen at the end of the story, then read the author's ending. After reading a story, close the book and help the child think up the idea for another story using the same characters. Keep the child's books where he can reach them. Teach the child the sounds of the various letters, and let him see the logical way in which these sounds are put together to say the entire word. Let him see you reading to yourself for enjoyment, and that will encourage him to enjoy reading also.

Some children will advance much more rapidly than these suggestions indicate, and as the children become older, the inherent pleasure of reading should begin to speed the process. With older children, make it possible for them to own their own books, taking advantage of movie tie-ins or the popularity of sports or entertainment personalities to whet their appetites to read. Try to budget money for the inexpensive paperback books offered in school book clubs—you will never spend the money more profitably than to buy for a child a book he chooses and is eager to read.

The most important thing for elementary and junior high children is not necessarily the intellectual quality of what they choose to read but that they are reading something. If a child sees that by reading he can learn something related to his own interests, something he cannot learn any other way, the battle of making him into a reader is half won. Far better for a fifth grader to read eagerly a simple book about Michael Jackson or the Boston Red Sox than for him to slog grudgingly through a classic of children's literature that bores him. Help him find things to read that are life related and entertaining, and as he grows older and his interests become more refined, his choice of reading material will reflect it.

Children will learn best to do those things that have some immediate connection to what is happening in their lives at that particular time. In Tennessee Williams's play *This Property Is Condemned,* one of the characters explained why he had no use for the academic life: "I quituated school four years ago 'cause they was teachin' algebra, and I didn't give a damn what 'X' stood for."

There is a message there that every parent should keep in mind: if basic learning skills seem irrelevant to the daily concerns of the child, he will resist even the best strategies we use to teach him. And if, on the other hand, he learns that reading is fun and relevant to his here and now, almost nothing we do will *keep* him from reading.

22

Sports have always been an essential part of childhood development and are now more so than ever, as the number of organized athletic programs for youngsters increases each year. Today, thanks to changing attitudes and new federal regulations, hundreds of thousands of young girls who formerly watched from the sidelines are joining American boys in organized athletic competition.

As an indication of just how important kids' sports programs have become, consider this statistic: in boys' Little League programs, 1.8 million baseball games were played in the United States in 1983! This single organization sponsors 150,000 *teams* with over two and a half million youngsters playing on a regular basis. And Little League baseball is only a small part of the entire picture, of course. Some 927,000 kids strap on helmets and shoulder pads each year as members of junior and senior high school football teams, for example. And when one adds up the number of kids involved in other programs—Boys and Girls clubs, the community YM and YWCAs, as well as the YM and

YWHAs; individual sports such as basketball teams, soccer programs; tennis, swimming and gymnastics leagues—the sheer volume of juvenile sports action is staggering.

Next to the classroom itself, the ball fields and gymnasiums of America are the setting for more self-concept training—for better or for worse—than any other area. The elements are all present: the child is learning skills of increasing difficulty, in the presence of peers to whom he is constantly compared, under the supervision of adults who give feedback about the quality of his performance. It would be difficult to devise a situation more fertile for the growth of one's self-image, whether positive or negative.

Because organized sports creates such a potent and sometimes volatile opportunity for a child's emotional development, some psychologists question the wisdom of allowing young kids to participate at all. Horror stories abound of youngsters cracking under the pressure of big-time competition, unathletic children being emotionally crushed by harsh criticism from coaches who expect too much, and other such unhappy outcomes. Many parents conclude, quite reasonably, that organized sports is not worth the psychological risks for young children and avoid such programs altogether.

As an individual whose own self-esteem was enhanced by sports, and who as a coach saw hundreds of youngsters similarly affected, I bring to this argument a tendency to approve of athletics for youngsters. On the other hand, as a father who was not very temperate or balanced in managing my sons' athletic activities, and who has often seen outrageous parental behavior damage the spirit and self-esteem of young kids, I understand the negative side of sports as well.

But when the pros and cons are all weighed and

sifted, I have no ambivalence whatever about the over-all role of sports: I believe the positive potential of kids' athletics is so great that a parent is foolish not to take advantage of it. Handled properly, a child's involvement in sports can be a terrific tool for the teaching of self-esteem. A good parent should run, not walk, to the nearest sporting goods store and put a basketball, tennis racket, hockey stick, golf club, baseball bat, or something in his child's hand as soon as possible.

What do kids learn in sports? Apart from learning how to hit a ball or throw one, children learn several more important things:

• They learn teamwork.
• They learn how to deal with failure.
• They learn the role of attitude in performance.

Learning teamwork includes two components. Part of teamwork is learning that there are different roles to be played on a team, some of them more glamorous than others, and that all these roles are equally necessary for a winning team. This aspect of teamwork can be learned only by participation in team sports such as baseball, football, and basketball, and I recommend that every child be a part of at least one of these team sports. The role playing on an athletic team truly is a metaphor of life—it's not just a corny sports cliché. Everyone can't be a star on a team, but the contribution of all team members is necessary for the team to win, and that lesson must be learned by both the hero and the supporting cast. The quarterback gets the headlines, but if the guard doesn't block for him, nobody gets anything but lumps and bruises. That life-related principle is learned more readily in sports than in any other activity I am aware of.

There is another element of teamwork that is learned in athletics, and that is recognizing the opportunity for many different people to work for the common good, with the understanding that the team goal is more important than individual success. This part of teamwork can be learned not only in traditional team sports but also in sports such as tennis, golf, gymnastics, and swimming—sports in which each person's performance is individual, but the events themselves are organized around team competition.

A young girl on a gymnastics team learns to go out on the mat and perform her very best, and then sits with her teammates and roots for them to do even better so the team can win. A track athlete throws the discus as far as he can throw it, then cheers for his teammate to throw it farther. A tennis player discovers that winning any individual tennis match is much sweeter when his victory helps the entire team beat its opponent. In these kinds of sports, kids learn to appreciate the skills and abilities of others and to emphasize the common good over the individual achievement. That lesson is not learned as readily merely by shooting a basketball at a goal hanging over the garage at home.

Through sports, kids also learn how to deal with failure. Long-term success in anything requires times of temporary failure, and kids must learn to experience that kind of failure without giving up on themselves. Sports is full of temporary defeats. Baseball coaches are fond of pointing out to discouraged young batters that the immortal Babe Ruth got a hit only one-third of the times he went to the plate! The greatest golfers on the pro tour hit bad shots, have bad rounds, and occasionally fail to make the cut in major tournaments. Great athletes are those who bounce back from their temporary failures.

That basic lesson is learned quickly by a young athlete. He learns that he can't get a hit every time he goes to bat. He learns that he is going to get knocked down every so often, and when it happens, there is nothing to do but get up again and keep going. A youngster who participates in individual sports such as tennis or skiing, no matter how good he is, will occasionally run into someone who is better. With the help of a sensitive coach or parent, the child learns to put that realization into perspective, and it makes him a better athlete and a more balanced human being.

Another part of the young athlete's education is learning about the role of attitude in performance. It is no coincidence that so many of the illustrations and examples one reads in motivational books are taken from the world of sports. Athletic competition at any level, from the Olympic championships right down to Midget League football games, is rich with situations in which attitude and belief make a difference.

In sports the difference between winning and losing is easier to see than in most things; the feedback is immediate and the signs of self-confidence or self-doubt are unmistakable. In that setting, kids see and understand how important positive attitudes can be. They learn, even if only in a general and instinctive way, something about the dynamics of self-belief, the ebb and flow of emotional momentum, and the competitive edge that self-confidence gives—to all areas of life.

It has often been said that football builds character, and that is something of an overstatement; no sport truly teaches character, but it can teach a kid the habits of success. It can teach that hard work produces results, that perseverance pays off, that delayed gratification usually brings a reward worth the effort.

I was a good coach for ten years. I coached lots of winning teams and a few championship teams. I was successful not because I had the best technical understanding of basketball but because I understood that an average kid, self-confident and highly motivated, will beat a more talented but less motivated opponent every time. I was a good coach because as a young boy I was only an average athlete; if I had been a star myself, I don't think I would have been as good a coach. But I understood the not-so-talented boys; I knew where they were coming from, and I had compassion for them.

We won lots of ball games because I taught my boys that what wins ball games is not simply technical skills. Ball games are not won by X's and O's on a chalkboard. Ball games are won by kids who believe in themselves, kids who want to win more than their opponents do, kids who are so sure of ultimate victory that they refuse to quit. If a coach can teach a child how to be that kind of athlete, chances are good the child will continue to be that kind of person long after he is through playing ball. That is the best reason I know for a child to be involved in organized sports.

Of all the boys I coached, none is a better example of the positive influence of sports than a kid whose teammates nicknamed him "The Turtle."

Whatever the sport, having a nickname like Turtle is not a good sign! When I was an assistant football coach at West End High School in Birmingham, a young boy whose chances to play seemed remote tried out for the team. He was short and pudgy; he measured 5 feet 5 inches and weighed 160 pounds, but he looked even chubbier. Standing alongside the other boys, he looked like a physical misfit, and some of the coaches didn't want to waste equipment on him, but he insisted he wanted to play football, so was issued a uniform.

The boy's name was Billy Battle. As a freshman, he was moved to three or four different positions and used mostly as a human blocking dummy, but he never missed practice, he never complained, and he always gave his best. The second year, there was no significant progress. He was moved from tackle to center and then to end. He had grown a couple of inches, but he was still just a chubby kid who loved football.

Billy was so slow his teammates laughed at him. At the end of practice every day, the football players ran hundred-yard dashes as a conditioning drill, and Billy would always finish last, well behind everyone else. The other players would kneel on the goal line waiting for him to arrive, often chanting, "Come on, Turtle; come on, Turtle," as he chugged toward the finish line.

In his junior year, Billy continued to grow and started to get faster. In the middle of the season, another player was injured and Billy was put into the game as a defensive end. To the total amazement of all us coaches, he played a spectacular game and was named by a Birmingham newspaper as the "outstanding player of the week." He had a starting position for the rest of the season, and during that summer, he lifted weights, ran track to improve his speed, and worked to be ready for his senior year.

That fall, Billy Battle became one of the best high school football players I have ever seen. He emerged as the leader of our team, got better every week, was named all-city, all-state, and all-American at the end of the season, and was recruited by major universities all over the country. He went to the University of Alabama, where he became an outstanding lineman. He played in three major bowl games—the Cotton Bowl, Sugar Bowl, and Orange Bowl—and helped lead his Alabama team to a national championship.

The Turtle didn't stop there. After graduation, he served as an assistant coach at several colleges and, at the age of twenty-eight, became the head football coach of the University of Tennessee, the youngest

23

Although I strongly advocate the involvement of boys and girls in organized sports, I must caution that the rich potential of such involvement can easily be short-circuited by the wrong parental approach.

Most of the sins committed by parents in managing their child's athletic activity fall into the same category: excessive, overzealous involvement. Sports can become a negative experience for a child when his parents are too ambitious, too concerned with winning, and in too big a hurry for the child to reach higher levels of skill. All that adds up to excessive pressure on the child, and that means trouble.

I should know. When the hall of fame of athletically overzealous fathers is established, my name will be there. It is my shame, and I readily confess it: I pushed my boys into sports, too early and too hard, and I should have known better. I can only plead that when I saw the mistake I was making, I changed my approach and now preach against fanatical parents with the fervor of the reformed sinner.

Both my boys had a ball and bat in their hands by the time they could grasp. Billy, my oldest son, was born while I was still in college. Literally, by the time he learned to walk, I was trying to teach him how to do push-ups. Before he was three years old, he could swim distances of over a mile. Before he began school, I had him doing chin-ups on a specially built bar. I put a pint-sized basketball goal on the wall in my high school gym so he could learn to shoot and handle a basketball when he was five years old. I hate to admit it, but every time we entertained guests at our house, I would have Billy do push-ups to show off for our friends.

I was determined that my two boys were going to be the best little athletes in forty-six counties. I had them both throwing and batting a baseball when they were toddlers. I worked with them constantly, teaching them to switch-hit (I had heard Mickey Mantle's father did this), batting right-handed and left-handed, throwing hundreds of balls to them and hitting hundreds of balls for them to field.

The lowest point I reached was allowing Billy, at the age of five, to take batting practice against an all-state high school pitcher who threw the ball eighty-five to ninety miles an hour. I put little Billy up there at the plate with a bat in his hands to practice against that pitcher, and then fussed at him for backing out of the batter's box. He was afraid of the ball, of course, and I chided him for being afraid and told him he would never be a great hitter if he didn't learn to stand in there and face that ninety-mile-an-hour fastball!

Both Billy and Mike were so good that I couldn't wait for them to become six or seven years old so they could play Little League baseball. I conspired with a Little League coach to falsify their ages, and enable them to start playing a year before they reached the minimum age. Carolyn and I would go to their games, expecting them to get a hit every time they came to the plate; we wanted them never to make an out or a mistake.

My eyes were opened when I began attending those first Little League ball games. As I saw parents acting like total nincompoops, I began to reassess my own behavior. In the next few years, as I umpired hundreds of kids' ball games as a part-time summer job, I watched the enormous pressure put on these youngsters to perform perfectly. I saw them ridiculed, demeaned, and humiliated by coaches and parents.

I was eventually able to recognize my attitude toward Billy and Mike for what it was—an attempt to live my own life through them, a willingness to use them to indulge my own appetite for sports and for winning. I began to ease off, but I still regard that mistake as the worst I ever made as a father.

I, just as many fathers, have had to learn some fairly elementary lessons in my approach to my boys' sports:

• I had to learn that my two boys were different. They matured at different rates, enjoyed different types of sports, and had different attitudes toward competition. I couldn't accept this at first. Because Billy liked football, I expected Mike to like football, and put pressure on him to play high school ball without ever finding out if it was what he really wanted. I just assumed he liked football, because Billy did, and that was a mistake.

• I had to learn that kids will be kids, and sometimes they simply don't want to play a highly structured and intensely competitive sport. Sometimes they want to just play, and as kids they should be allowed to do so without being treated like losers of some sort.

When I was in graduate school at the University of Alabama, the head tennis coach at the university became a personal friend of mine and offered to give my boys tennis lessons. I was delighted; this was a great opportunity for them, I thought. We went to K mart, bought two tennis rackets and some cheap tennis shoes, and took the boys to the campus tennis courts for their lessons. Tennis was to be the summer agenda for Billy and Mike. But neither of them wanted to play. They wanted, instead, to wade in the creek behind our house and catch crawdads and minnows.

I was furious with them. This was such a perfect chance to learn tennis, but they fussed and complained. It was too hot, they said, and besides they wanted to play in the creek. This upset me so badly that I laid down the law: "You will go out there and you will learn to play tennis and you will enjoy it!" At this stage, Carolyn, with the superior wisdom of a mother, intervened. She pointed out, that among other things, the temperature was 100 to 110 degrees every day, that Mike and Billy were little boys, and that little boys like to play in creeks in the summertime. She won the debate.

• I had to learn to let my children make their own decisions about sports, and to respect those decisions. A child who is involved in the game *he* wants to play, rather than the game his parents want him to play, will almost inevitably play it better and learn more from it. In an ironic twist, Mike taught me this lesson when he decided he wanted to play, of all things, tennis.

Never mind that he wanted nothing to do with tennis when it was my idea; several years later, when I wanted him to play football, Mike wanted to play tennis. Although a late starter in the sport, he developed the love for the game that I hoped he would have, but that never developed, for football. It was almost as if he was determined to become good at the wrong sport!

And he did become good at it. He eventually went to the Sumter campus of the University of South Carolina on a tennis scholarship, he and his doubles partner reached the semi-finals of the junior college national tennis championships. After college, and he ranked in the top ten of the singles open division in the state of South Carolina. So it was a bit of poetic justice that, years after we had argued so fiercely over the creek and the crawdads, Mike insisted that I take up the sport of tennis so we could play together. I began playing, learned to love the game myself, and Mike and I became doubles partners, eventually reaching the finals in our first father-son tournament. We play doubles together often today, and I must say we are pretty tough to beat.

Mike and Billy both became what any sensible father hopes his sons will be—capable athletes who enjoy sports as part of well-balanced lives. But they arrived at that point in their own way, in their own time, playing the sports they chose to play. Considering the way I started them out, I will admit I got lucky.

For those parents who still are making the important decisions regarding your child's sports, radio sportscaster Jim Simpson has written Ten Commandments of Sports for Parents:

1. Make sure that your child knows that—win or lose, scared or heroic—you love him, appreciate his efforts, and are not disappointed in him.

2. Try your best to be completely honest about your child's athletic capability, his competitive attitude, his sportsmanship, and his actual skill level.

3. Be helpful . . . but don't coach him on the way to the rink, track, or court . . . or on the way back . . . or at breakfast.

4. Teach him to enjoy the thrill of competition. Don't say, "Winning doesn't count," because it does.

5. Try not to relive your athletic life through your child in a way that creates pressure. Don't pressure him because of *your* pride.

6. Don't compete with the coach. Remember, in many cases, the coach is a hero to his athletes, a person who can do no wrong.

7. Don't compare the skill, courage, or attitudes of your child with that of other members of the squad or team.

8. Get to know the coach so you can be sure that his philosophy, attitude, ethics, and knowledge are such that you are happy to expose your child to him.

9. Always remember that children tend to exaggerate, both when praised and when criticized. Temper your reactions when they bring home tales of woe or heroics.

10. Make a point of understanding courage and the fact that it is relative. Some of us climb mountains but fear a fight; some of us fight but turn to jelly if a bee buzzes nearby. A child must know: courage is not *absence* of fear, but, rather, doing something *in spite of* fear.

24

Nothing a parent can teach his child is more important than having the ability to set goals and reach them.

Ultimately, high self-esteem must be supported by tangible evidence of personal achievement. Parents and teachers can be tireless boosters of the child's self-image, but at some point none of that is adequate; eventually, the child must experience for himself the pride of taking on a tough task and accomplishing it. That experience will accelerate the development of his self-esteem more rapidly than a thousand bumper stickers.

When a child sets a goal and reaches it, his achievement sets into motion a benign spiral: the success makes him feel better about himself, which helps him to achieve more, which makes him feel better about himself, and on and on. . . .

There is no better way to engage the child in this positive cause-and-effect sequence than to teach him to set goals. Every child has many wants and wishes, and these comprise an abundant supply of raw material from which his goals may be fashioned. Beginning with those personal desires of the child, teach him to set goals, using the following steps:

- Determine what things he really wants.
- Write these down in order of priority.
- Identify the obstacles.
- Set specific target dates.
- Visualize the completed goal.
- Get excited. Act as if the goal is reached.
- Use positive affirmations.

This simple process is a useful way for children, as well as adults, to approach personal goal setting. If the child can be shown that such a process leads to the attainment of one's wishes, he learns one of life's most basic lessons—that rewards are linked to behavior, that what one gets in life is inextricably bound to what one does.

This process can be applied to children of any age. The parent can sit down with the child and tell him explicitly: "Let's talk about how people get what they want." List these seven steps and explain each step to the child, then offer to work with the child in applying the process in some particular instance. The most obvious time to do this is when the child is asking for something that is beyond what he might normally expect to be given—a new designer-label outfit, for example, for a twelve-year-old daughter. The advantage of starting in this way is that you are beginning with a priority she has established for herself. The fuel that powers all goal reaching is strong individual desire, and the parent must be sure that such desire is present before trying to demonstrate goal setting to the child.

Letting children establish their own goals is essential not only to their ability to learn goal setting but also to the more general learning of self-esteem. Psychiatrist Jerome L. Schulman says that by the age of nine a youngster should be making 50 percent of the decisions affecting his life. Too often a parent tries to teach his child how to reach goals that are not really the child's goals at all, but are rather goals that the parent has maneuvered the child into making. When this is the case, the most critical element of the process—an intense desire for the goal/object—is missing, and the attempt frequently fails.

In selecting a goal, it is important that the child choose something that is within his reach, so in this the parent must sometimes exert some influence. If the goal is too easily reached, of course, the entire process is seen as an empty exercise. But a goal that is too difficult, or requires the child's attention over too long a period of time, is also counterproductive. The parent must help the child select a goal that can be realized with a reasonable amount of work over a relatively short period of time.

In selecting the goal, it is also important that the child not choose something that is competitive in nature, some goal that depends upon outperforming someone else for its realization. When a child sets as his goal being the first-chair clarinet player in the seventh-grade band, for example, or winning the hundred-yard dash in the annual school field day, reaching that goal depends on the child's performance relative to other children and is thus a poor choice for teaching goal setting. The child may do all he can do, faithfully perform all the intermediate steps toward the goal, and still not get the payoff. Such competitive risks are common in real-life goal setting, of course, but when a child is young, it is important that he be encouraged to set goals that depend entirely upon his own performance.

To recap, the child should be helped to choose a goal

that is (1) truly his own, (2) within his reach, and (3) not dependent on how his performance compares with that of another child.

Once the goal is set, teach the child the habit of stating the goal explicitly. It is important that the child understand the value of recognizing one's wants, of identifying and openly stating, "This is something I want, and I am going to get it by doing the following things. . . ." This is a healthy process for the child. It teaches him the more general habit of self-analysis, of getting in touch with his own feelings, as well as facilitates the achievement of the goal itself.

Clearly stating one's goal might include putting up visible reminders of it around the house—in the child's room or on the bathroom mirror or refrigerator door. A small card on which the goal is written, or a picture of the goal, serves as a public statement of intent to the family that the goal has been established, as well as a daily reminder to the child himself.

After the goal is established, the next step is to identify the intermediate behaviors that will lead to the goal. A meaningful goal is distinguished from mere wishful thinking by the presence of specific steps that lead to its fulfillment. The child must learn that if he does A, B, and C, the inevitable outcome will be X, which is the fulfillment of the goal itself. The parent must teach him to ask, "What must I do in order to get from where I am now to where I want to be?"

Once such a series of intermediate steps is arrived at, the goal becomes less an object of wishful thinking and more a tangible reward for some specific kinds of behavior. The child sees that the attainment of the goal is dependent on his own actions, rather than on the fates, the whims of his parents, or other such vague variables.

For this reason, good goals for teaching children

often involve some material object that can be acquired by earning a particular amount of money. The suitability of such a goal is obvious: the child can select something (a new toy, an article of clothing, or the like) that he personally would enjoy but that he is unlikely to be given; the attainment of that desire is not dependent on competitive success in any way; the amount of work (i.e., money) needed to reach the goal is predetermined and easily understood.

So the twelve-year-old girl who wants that trendy new outfit is helped to approach her wish in this fashion: "There is something I want. I decide I want it and say so. I identify the steps I must take to get it. I set dates for reaching those intermediate steps. I do things to remind myself of what I am working for. I think about how it will be when I have that outfit, and when I get tired and would rather be doing other things, I remember how good I will look in my new outfit. When I have done those things, I will have the outfit, so getting it or not getting it is up to me, not my parents or anyone else."

The process requires that the child have an available way of earning the money to acquire the goal/object. With young children, this can be done by assigning "pay" to tasks around the house. With older children, more substantive jobs such as baby-sitting or mowing lawns may be useful, but with today's economy and tight labor situation parents may find it necessary to contrive income-producing activities even for teen-agers.

Rather than allowing the child to set goals so directly tied to dollars and cents, the parent may choose to establish within the family a system of rewards that serves the same purpose. For example, a friend of mine has had great success with a point system with his three preteen children. In his system, certain specific goals (a new bicycle, video games, special trips) are assigned a certain number of points. One hundred points might be established as a fair rate for a new baseball mitt.

At the outset, points are also assigned to certain behaviors: two points for a clean room each morning when the child leaves for school, one point for every half hour of trumpet practice, three points for special jobs such as taking out the trash or vacuuming the carpets, five points for reading any book from a specified set, and so on.

The value of this system is clear: (1) it demonstrates the relationship between the things we get and the things we do; (2) it motivates the child to do things that are in themselves constructive, apart from the goal; (3) it takes the child's focus off the generosity of the parent and puts it on his own performance; and (4), most importantly, it closely approximates the way life works in the real world.

In order to start the child on the way to his objective, the parent might help him to find a picture of the baseball mitt he wants, or one like it, in a magazine, newspaper, or catalog. He might cut it out and post it on his bedroom wall or bathroom mirror, perhaps with the number of points written alongside it. If, in fact, his desire for the mitt is a fleeting whim, he will lose interest altogether, and a new goal should be selected. But even in such a case, the exercise has not been wasted. The child can see that his failure to get the mitt occurred because he didn't want it badly enough to do what was necessary to get it—rather than because he has stingy and ungenerous parents.

It may be useful to join your child in such a program of goal setting. Select a goal of your own and assign yourself certain point values for "work" you do around the house. Place your own tally card for points in a prominent place alongside your child's, and your own picture of your goal. This makes a game of goal setting for the young child and allows you to model as well as teach the process. The child can see that parents, too, are rewarded only after certain intermediate steps are achieved—an important lesson for children, who usually feel that adults somehow are able to produce magically whatever *they* really want.

An important part of the goal-reaching process is "self-talk," the use of the power of suggestion in one's own mental conversations with oneself.

Every child who has read *The Little Engine That Could* is already acquainted with self-talk. Children should be taught that the lessons of the story are applicable to any task or challenge. The little train that chugs "I think I can; I think I can" as it strains to cross the mountain peak is a prototype of the self-affirming positive thinker, and children are never too young to learn to engage in such self-talk.

Everyone engages in self-suggestion, whether he realizes it or not. The "stream of consciousnes" that flows through our minds is an important part of our attitudinal conditioning, and the more positive such thoughts are, the better. Dale Carnegie once said, "Is giving yourself a pep talk every day silly, superficial, and childish? No! On the contrary, it is the very essence of sound psychology."

Psychologists Donald W. Felker and Susan Bahlke Thomas did a study on self-talk in nine-year-olds and reported that children with high self-concepts indicated that they made positive statements about themselves while doing schoolwork, while those with low self-concept—and low achievement—did not do so.

Children who learn that talking positively to oneself is not foolish have learned a valuable lesson that can last a lifetime.

A young athlete in one of the Sumter County high schools taught me a fresh lesson in the value of self-suggestion. He was one of fourteen children and was physically rather small, but he had a goal—to play college football. He spoke to me one day when I was visiting his high school: "Dr. Mitchell, I want you to know that I have really utilized the tool of self-suggestion every day and every night for the past year and a half, and it has made a change in my life. I am convinced that even though the colleges think I'm too small to play, and not one of them has offered me a scholarship, I am going to a major college and I am going to make it."

He told me that that was his goal, and for many months, every morning and night and in between, he had repeated that affirmation to himself: "I am not too small; I can play college ball; I am going to make it!"

And he did make it. He went to Clemson University as a "walk-on," with no scholarship or spot on the football team. He tried out for the team his freshman year, failed to make it, and tried again his sophomore year. That year, his persistent self-talk paid off: he made the team and became a contributing member of the Clemson Tiger squad that went on to win a national championship.

25

The outstanding results of the PMA program in District Two did not end in Sumter County.

As we watched the remarkable developments of our students and teachers in Sumter during those years, a dream emerged; we began to envision the benefits of positive thinking being extended to the sixteen thousand or so school systems cross the United States.

The first glimmer that such a dream would someday be realized came while the Sumter project was still under way. School districts throughout South Carolina and other states began asking for assistance in beginning a PMA program in their districts. As our efforts received national media attention (Paul Harvey, for example, devoted part of a network television show to the program), my staff and I gradually allocated more and more time to answering inquiries about the project. School superintendents, principals, and teachers came to Sumter from as far away as Colorado to observe what we were doing in District Two.

Dr. Norman Vincent Peale, during his visit to

Sumter, had predicted such a development. His response to our program had been enthusiastically supportive, and on a television show, he made the following statement in regard to the PMA program: "I am on the road about three or four days a week. I have spoken in every state in the United States; never at any place have I encountered a positive thinking program as well thought out, as scientifically executed and in as great depth as I find here." Later, he told me personally that he believed what we were doing could "change the course of public education" throughout the entire nation.

We stayed in touch with Dr. Peale after his visit to Sumter, and he was very encouraging to me and other public school administrators when we decided to establish a nonprofit foundation that would help school systems throughout the world in implementing the PMA program.

Dr. Jim Melvin, former superintendent of schools in Whitfield County, Georgia, and presently superintendent of schools in Fort Myers, Florida, expressed a view I heard from many other educators. He traveled to Sumter to see our program for himself and, at the end of the visit, he told me, "Bill, this is a great program. It's what is needed in school systems across this country. But I need help in getting started, and I know the other superintendents with whom I've talked need help also. Isn't there any way you could be available to help people like us do what you've done here?"

The answer turned out to be yes, and the opportunity to organize such a foundation came sooner than I expected. In early 1981, I found myself in a conflict with some of the members of my school board over one of the school system's employees. A few politically influential board members insisted that I dismiss a staff member for reasons I felt were unfounded and unfair.

We reached an impasse over the matter, and it became a divisive and emotional local issue. Rather than fire the staff member for what I thought were unjustifiable reasons, I resigned the District Two superintendency.

It was a painful episode for me, personally and professionally, but the cloud had a silver lining: it gave me, quite unexpectedly, a year away from the daily demands of a superintendency. I committed that year to my dream—that once-distant goal of organizing a national foundation for teaching educators how to put attitude-training programs into their schools.

Dr. Peale graciously consented to meet with my wife, Carolyn, and me in Pawling, New York, and it was there that we shared with him our intent to help school systems in all parts of the country to implement a systematic program for developing self-worth in their students and employees. School systems from thirty-five states had previously sent representatives to Sumter to see our program, or had written to request information. Several of them had implemented the PMA program based on our verbal or written communications with them. Selecting from among the many inquiries we had received, we chose ten systems—choosing a variety of sizes and locations—and invited the superintendents to a meeting in Atlanta at the beginning of 1982.

Traveling at their own expense, over the Christmas–New Year holiday break, all ten superintendents came to Atlanta. They represented states as different from one another as Alabama, Utah, and Ohio—from school systems as varied as Whitfield County, Georgia, or Jefferson County (Louisville), Kentucky, to small rural systems in Virginia and Pennsylvania. The Atlanta meeting was a historic bench mark for positive thinking. For the first time, the chief executive officers of a diverse group of school systems came together to support a systematic effort to improve the attitudes of students.

From that meeting came the support for the national foundation of which we had dreamed: the Power of Positive Students (POPS) International Foundation, which was officially chartered later that year. The purpose of the POPS Foundation is to provide to superintendents and principals the expertise, tools, and consultants needed to set into motion the positive-thinking program in their school districts.

In the next several months, influential Birmingham businessmen such as Hugh Jacks and Joe Steeley learned about the POPS Foundation and lent their backing to it. A permanent national office was established in Birmingham, and Dr. M. Gardner McCollum, a nationally known curriculum specialist from the University of Alabama, took a sabbatical leave from his faculty duties to serve as its first full-time executive director.

Today, the POPS Foundation is gaining momentum as more and more school systems seek creative solutions to the tasks they face. School systems in more than twenty-five states are using the POPS program, and requests for assistance and information regarding the program have been received from all fifty states.

Evidence is piling up that the POPS approach works, not just in Sumter or a few isolated school systems with special problems but in all types of schools all across the country. As the program goes into effect in more places, we are hearing of a wider range of benefits than even we imagined might be possible. Here is a sample of some of the results reported to us:

• A school in Colorado Springs, Colorado, reports that graffiti on its walls, once a major problem, has virtually disappeared since the POPS program began there, and that playground fights have declined from six to ten incidents per day to a low of two to three *per month* currently.

• The Salt Lake City, Utah, school system, after a year in the POPS program, reports that student referrals to juvenile agencies that normally averaged 120 per year dropped to under 70. In the area of employer-employee relations, the number of teacher grievances filed dropped from eighteen in the previous year to four.

• The Tyrone, Pennsylvania, school system reports that, for the second straight year, bus suspensions for student misbehavior have been less than 50 percent of the pre-POPS level, and that acts of vandalism have also decreased dramatically.

• A high school principal in Wilmington, Delaware, reports that since instituting the POPS program, "It is a great feeling to see people getting excited about school." Attendance at his school has increased from 79 percent to over 90 percent. The football team, which had won only six games in the previous six years, has made "a complete turnaround by winning the Flight B championship and representing our district in the state play-offs!"

• The Windward, Kaneohe, Hawaii, district superintendent stated that after a year of using the POPS program, there were positive measurable results pertaining to student achievement in both academic and nonacademic areas and notable improved relationships among employees.

• In Dalton, Georgia, the county school superintendent writes, "We have been named one of the top ten school systems in the state of Georgia, and there is no doubt that the POPS program was one of the major contributing factors. Students, teachers, and all our employees feel better about themselves."

• In Pleasants County, West Virginia, after the

board of education approved the implementation of the POPS program, the school system had 130 out of a possible 134 total compliances from an on-site review board—the best performance of any system in the state.

• A middle school principal from Scottsdale, Arizona, reports that "use of the POPS tools has produced observable results in student behavior and interactions." (He also notes that he was the recipient of the Outstanding Educator of the Year award and believes the POPS program was the key to his success.)

• From Rock Island, Illinois, a superintendent describes a generally improved atmosphere in the schools. As evidence, he reports that the students in one of his schools recently had a surprise party simply to tell their principal how much they appreciate him!

As I have traveled to school systems across the country, I have seen dozens of indications of that improved emotional climate of which the Illinois administrator writes. In schools where POPS principles are taught, people seem to care more for one another, or at least to express their positive feelings more freely. The positive atmosphere affects everyone in the school, from the principal to the smallest first grader or the custodial staff.

While visiting a school in Pennsylvania recently, I noticed the food service workers had put up signs with bright, cheerful slogans around the lunchroom. I watched these ladies dish out the food to the youngsters with smiles and encouraging words, and saw how many of the children smiled back and thanked the workers. The environment of that lunchroom was so positive, it practically radiated good feelings. I talked with the lunchroom manager, and she said that since POPS began in their school, there had been "an absolutely unbelievable difference in these kids!" Among the many intangible differences were a couple of tangible ones that perhaps only a lunchroom manager would notice: since POPS, she said, there was less food being thrown away, and much less silverware lost or stolen!

26

After a year away from duty as a practicing administrator, I was eager to return to the front lines of the educational wars. As exciting as it had been to create the POPS Foundation, the challenge of a real-life public school system has always been powerfully attractive to me. In the summer of 1982, I accepted a position as superintendent of schools in the western Maryland town of Cumberland. I am presently superintendent of the Allegany County public school system, once again facing the daily tasks of running a public school district.

My first priority, wherever I go, is to create a more positive emotional environment, and it has been rewarding to see that such an effort is paying off in Allegany County just as it did in South Carolina. The old cliché is that positive thinking begins at home, and we have tried to make our school system a model of what can happen when students, parents, educators, and the community engage in an effort of mutual support and affirmation.

In the two years since we began emphasizing POPS

principles in Allegany County, we have seen numerous areas in which the improved attitudes and sense of self-worth are paying off:

- *Attendance.* Pupil attendance in the state of Maryland as a whole is not good; the state recently ranked forty-third among the fifty states, with a 91 percent pupil attendance average. Allegany County's pupil attendance average of 94.5 percent was the highest in the state in 1984.

- *Suspensions.* In our school system, student suspensions have dropped from 501 suspensions in 1981 to 410 in 1984. We have a current rate of 6 percent suspensions in Allegany County as compared to 26 percent in the state as a whole.

- *Drop-out rate.* Providing students with a sense of self-worth affects their drop-out rate as much as any other single statistic. In Allegany County, our annual drop-out rate is only 1.3 percent, compared to a statewide rate of 4.1 percent.

- *"Holding power."* We use this phrase to describe the ability of a school system to keep its kids in the classroom through graduation, and measure it as the percentage of ninth graders who graduate four years later. In the 1982–83 school year, we set a new record in "holding power" in Allegany County, with 89.7 percent and, in 1983–84, broke that record with a 93.8 percent rating.

- *Parent involvement.* A good index of the degree to which parents are catching the vision of any positive-thinking program is parents' willingness to spend time in the schools as volunteer workers. In previous years in Allegany County, the highest number of parents involved as volunteers was 1,181; since the POPS program began in 1982–83, we have placed a new emphasis on the parents' role in the schools and, last year, had 3,940 parents enrolled as volunteer workers!

• *Drug and alcohol abuse.* In the past two years from 1982 to 1984, referrals for alcohol abuse have decreased from twenty-four cases annually to ten. Drug-related incidents among our students have dropped from sixteen cases to twelve. (This is with a total student enrollment in excess of twelve thousand.)

• *Employee grievances.* We have over fifteen hundred employees in our system and from 1982 to 1984, had only seventeen grievances, the lowest number ever in a two-year period. Of that number, only seven went to arbitration.

The point of all these data is not to depict the Allegany County system as a faultless, trouble-free school district. As public school systems go, it is fairly typical, with its normal share of assets and liabilities, with certain advantages and certain disadvantages over other systems. What is important is that the principles of self-esteem and attitude training that worked so well in Sumter County are working equally well in the quite different geographic and cultural situation offered in Allegany County. In each case, it is the principles, not the particular town or the particular teachers and students, that have made the difference.

The amazing results of the POPS program experienced in schools and communities all over the country can occur in every home and school system in which the need exists for a more positive, more hopeful, more caring emotional environment. The goal of our program is to show that it can happen anywhere; we can teach our children success as surely as we can teach them biology and math. To do so, we must be willing to invest time and resources in the effort to show them that everybody is somebody special.

Pablo Casals, Spanish-born cellist, conductor, and

composer, clearly was not an educator, but surely he knew something about success, and about the human spirit. Perhaps he said it best:

> What do we teach our children in school? We teach them that two plus two are four and that Paris is the capital of France. When will we also teach them what they are? We should say to each of them: "Do you know what you are? You are a marvel. You are unique. In all the world there is no other child exactly like you. In the millions of years that have passed, there has never been a person like you. You may become a Shakespeare, a Michelangelo, a Beethoven. You have the capacity for anything!"

Somehow, growing up in the steel mill towns of Alabama, I learned something of that feeling of self-worth that Casals so eloquently described. In my case, there was no organized POPS program in the schools I attended, no positive-thinking rallies or motivational billboards in town. But that essential ingredient to a child's self-esteem, the loving attention of significant adults, was there when I needed it, and it made all the difference.

The challenge of our schools and homes should be to insure that such an ingredient is available to every youngster. If a "little" Billy Mitchell with cardboard in his shoes can become a successful school administrator—one who currently speaks and serves as a consultant in school systems all over this country and one who has had the privilege of sitting with United States senators, four-star generals, presidents of corporations, millionaires, and Olympic gold-medal winners—then any boy or girl in America today can become a productive, positive adult. What's needed is someone to intervene in time—as Mrs. McIndoe, Coach Minto, and Sergeant Lacey did for me. Personalities such as Bob Hope, Zig Ziglar, Norman Vincent Peale, Bob Richards, and Bill Raspberry all have told me personally that they, likewise, attribute much of their success to encouragement given them by significant others.

My primary mission in life is to inspire others to develop their potential and believe in themselves. Why? Because each one of us deserves to be the best he can be. My second goal is to remind parents that our children deserve to be encouraged frequently.

The molding of a child's attitude is one of those areas in which one person—one parent, one teacher, one neighbor who takes an interest in teaching a child that he is a person of value—can make a big difference.

We cannot reasonably regard this task as being optional; it may well be that it is our best and last hope for stopping the erosion of public education in the United States. According to a 1983 report by the National Council for Educational Reform, the problems of public education are not being solved by the conventional approaches. Nationwide, the statistics are staggering:

• Twenty-three million American adults are functionally illiterate.

• About 13 percent of all seventeen-year-olds are functionally illiterate, and that figure may run as high as 40 percent among minority youth.

• Average achievement of high school students on standardized tests is now lower than twenty-five years ago.

• More than half the gifted students do not match their ability with comparable school achievement.

The time has come in America for parents and educators to do something about the low self-esteem that lies at the heart of such a dismal educational outlook. To teach children the enormous power of their own attitudes should be the highest goal of education. They will not learn how great is their potential unless we teach them.

When Confucius was asked to describe the most beautiful sight in the world, he answered, "The most beautiful sight in the world is a little child going confidently down the road after you have shown him the way." We who are parents are the teachers of life. We have an opportunity to enjoy that "most beautiful sight" multiplied many times over as we show those we love most that they are designed for lives of happiness and success.

ACKNOWLEDGMENTS

I give special thanks to God for providing me with the courage to persist throughout the tough times, and I am profoundly grateful to my wife, Carolyn, and our two wonderful sons, Billy and Michael, who have been a limitless source of inspiration and encouragement to me.

I would also like to express my deepest gratitude and appreciation to the many wonderful people who have given so unselfishly of their time, talents, and energy to help make this book a reality:

- Bruce Sherrill, Sidney Johnson, Billy Malone, Wilbur Moore, and the late Robert Allen, the members of the Board of Education in Alabama that granted me my first superintendency;
- the members of the greatest school board ever assembled—C. C. "Red" Berry, Glen Turbyville, Howard Sloan, Tom Kennedy, and John Ed McQueen;
- Guy Dyke, E. M. Watt, Henry Jackson, and Furman Avin, Sumter school board members

who believed in me and in the need for a positive-thinking program in public schools. For their active assistance in implementing the program in Sumter School District II, I give special thanks;

- Dr. R. Neil Williams, Mary M. Robb, R. Margaret Hamilton, George K. Conway, and the late O. Delbert Proudfoot, school board members in Allegany County who encouraged me to "spread the good news" across the country;
- the Reverend Tilford Junkins, my childhood pastor, who knew how to lift a person's spirits and remind him he was made in the image of God.

And my heartfelt gratitude to the friends and colleagues who have supported me:

- Estelle Hill, my former secretary, who always encouraged me to press on;
- Joe Steeley, a businessman in Birmingham, Alabama, who provided the financial means necessary to make the "POPS" International Foundation a reality;
- Hugh Jacks, William R. Battle III, Dr. M Donald Thomas, and Patricia Lindsey, who so capably served on the first board of directors of the "POPS" International Foundation;
- Dr. M. Gardner McCollum, a professor of education at the University of Alabama at Birmingham, who gave so generously of his time and talents to the "POPS" Foundation and served as its first executive director;
- Drs. Albert and Rachael Bickley, educational psychologists in South Carolina, who assisted in collecting and compiling the educational re-

search on which the "POPS" program is founded;

- Susan Meade, a secretary at the University of Alabama at Birmingham, who typed the first draft of the manuscript and many pages of research;
- Joe Pinner of WIS-TV, Columbia, South Carolina, who enthusiastically supported the "POPS" program from the beginning;
- Helen B. Dickerhoof, my administrative assistant and one of the most talented people God ever created.

To Dr. Norman Vincent Peale, who inspired me to stretch my abilities, I extend special thanks.

I would also like to thank my collaborator, Dr. Charles Paul Conn.

In closing, I would be remiss if I did not take this opportunity to thank the superintendents, principals, and teachers in the school systems across the country using the "Power of Positive Students" program.